Donated from

# The Trust Imperative

## Performance Improvement through Productive Relationships

Also available from ASQ Quality Press:

*The Change Agents' Handbook: A Survival Guide for Quality Improvement Champions*
David W. Hutton

*Performance Measurement Explained: Designing and Implementing Your State-of-the-Art System*
Bjørn Andersen and Tom Fagerhaug

*High Quality Leadership: Practical Guidelines to Becoming a More Effective Manager*
Erwin Rausch and John B. Washbush

*Let's Work Smarter, Not Harder: How to Engage Your Entire Organization in the Execution of Change*
Michael Caravatta

*Value Leadership: Winning Competitive Advantage in the Information Age*
Michael C. Harris

*Creativity, Innovation, and Quality*
Paul E. Plsek

*Managing Change: Practical Strategies for Competitive Advantages*
Kari Tuominen

*Root Cause Analysis: Simplified Tools and Techniques*
Bjørn Andersen and Tom Fagerhaug

To request a complimentary catalog of ASQ Quality Press publications, call 800-248-1946, or visit our website at http://qualitypress.asq.org .

# The Trust Imperative

## Performance Improvement through Productive Relationships

Stephen Hacker
Marsha Willard

with Laurent Couturier

ASQ Quality Press
Milwaukee, Wisconsin

*The Trust Imperative: Performance Improvement through Productive Relationships*
Stephen Hacker, Marsha Willard with Laurent Couturier

**Library of Congress Cataloging-in-Publication Data**

Hacker, Stephen, 1955–
  The trust imperative : performance improvement through productive
relationships / Stephen Hacker, Marsha Willard with Laurent Couturier.
    p. cm.
  Includes bibliographical references and index.
  ISBN 0-87389-527-4
  1. Organizational behavior. 2. Trust. 3. Interpersonal relations.
  I. Willard, Marsha L. II. Couturier, Laurent. III. Title.

HD58.7 .H33 2001
658—dc21                                                                    2001005599

© 2002 by ASQ

All rights reserved. No part of this book may be reproduced in any form or by any
means, electronic, mechanical, photocopying, recording, or otherwise, without the
prior written permission of the publisher.

10  9  8  7  6  5  4  3

ISBN 0-87389-527-4

Acquisitions Editor: Annemieke Koudstaal
Project Editor: Craig S. Powell
Production Administrator: Gretchen Trautman
Special Marketing Representative: David Luth

ASQ Mission: The American Society for Quality advances individual,
organizational, and community excellence worldwide through learning,
quality improvement, and knowledge exchange.

Attention Bookstores, Wholesalers, Schools, and Corporations: ASQ Quality
Press books, videotapes, audiotapes, and software are available at quantity
discounts with bulk purchases for business, educational, or instructional use.
For information, please contact ASQ Quality Press at 800-248-1946, or write to
ASQ Quality Press, P.O. Box 3005, Milwaukee, WI 53201-3005.

To place orders or to request a free copy of the ASQ Quality Press Publications
Catalog, including ASQ membership information, call 800-248-1946. Visit our
Web site at www.asq.org or http://qualitypress.asq.org .

Printed in the United States of America

 Printed on acid-free paper

**American Society for Quality**

Quality Press
600 N. Plankinton Avenue
Milwaukee, Wisconsin 53203
Call toll free 800-248-1946
Fax 414-272-1734
www.asq.org
http://qualitypress.asq.org
http://standardsgroup.asq.org
E-mail: authors@asq.org

# Dedications

*To the memory of my parents, Eddy and Peggy Hacker.*
*Their constant love and support gave me fertile*
*ground to grow and reach.*

Stephen Hacker

*To my children, Ana and Ava Mikolavich,*
*who teach me about trust every day.*

Marsha Willard

# Table of Contents

# Foreword

Who do you trust the most? Why? Who do you distrust? Why? As a psychologist I find it fascinating that everyone understands these questions and can answer them without much effort. The explanations about "why" often bring out strong feelings based on memorable experiences.

Trust is very important in our lives, yet "building trust" is seldom mentioned in statements of personal and organizational goals. It needs to be.

When I ask myself who I trust the most, the first person who comes to mind is my sister. Throughout our lives she has shown that I can trust her to not disclose private matters that I reveal to her in confidence and that I can absolutely count on her to do whatever she has promised she will do. I trust her so much that I had my attorney create a document giving her legal power to make decisions on my behalf if something would happen that renders me unconscious. I trust her with my life and all my possessions.

You have probably heard someone say "I'd trust him with my life." It's a good feeling when you can say it about someone you know and very good to hear someone say it about you. I had that kind of mutual bond years ago with a buddy in the army—made all the better because he was a Special Forces ranger.

Do you have that kind of deep feeling of trust in any of your relationships? How much do you trust the people you work with? How much do you trust your employer? Contractors? How much do you trust people you don't know very well, but whose actions affect your life?

When people are asked who they don't trust, why is it that used car salesmen and politicians come out high on the list? Most people explain that they can't trust used car salesmen and politicians to be fully truthful.

Several interesting issues emerge here. We have the strongest sense of trust with individuals who we know well and through their actions have created the feeling that they are trustworthy. It is easiest to distrust a group of people that we don't know personally, has been found in some instances to not be fully truthful, and has a reputation for manipulating people in unethical ways.

For ourselves, trustworthiness starts with the people we know best. From there our reputation gradually spreads. A principle to keep in mind is that it takes a long time to create feelings of trust in others, but a very short while to create distrust. It is also true that someone may be forgiven once for lying, cheating, or deceiving, but not usually twice.

People who have addictions will plead to be forgiven and ask for one more chance even though they cannot be trusted. Psychologists recommend that they should be made to earn trust through their actions. The depth of the emotional wound from feeling betrayed will vary from person to person. Some people forgive more easily and are more resilient than others.

Another principle is that we judge other people by their actions, but ourselves by our intentions. Some executives assume that their explanation about why they had to not be truthful about certain actions should be accepted, and are then perplexed when their employees do not trust them in future matters.

A few years ago a large corporation laid off hundreds of professional people who averaged about 20 years working for the company. After a year of good efforts to help them all find new jobs, there were still about 100 who were not reemployed. Psychologist James Pennebaker was brought in to work with them. He discovered that most of the ones still unemployed had received job offers, but they still had such strong feelings of betrayal that when they came close to being hired they would have an emotional reaction: What if I can't trust this employer either? Because they had not recovered from their emotional wounds, they were very distrustful.

A truth about human beings is that some people are very fearful of getting hurt and feel distrustful because they can't handle disruptive change very well. The real issue for them is not that their employer is untrustworthy, the problem is that they can't cope well with setbacks. They blame others for their distress and feel like victims. Fragile people have very little trust, while trust is not a big issue for highly resilient people who quickly find new directions for themselves.

It is clear that trusting everyone in all situations is not smart. Nor is it wise to distrust all people and all situations. The goal is to become conscious about when to trust and when to be cautious, considering the amount of risk.

I'm delighted to see many insights and guidelines in this book on how to develop trust. Using it you can learn skills for developing trust in others, and trustworthiness in yourself, and create a high trust organization.

Al Siebert, Ph.D., author of *The Survivor Personality*

# Acknowledgments

The learnings and ideas expressed in this book were shaped by the input of many valued colleagues. We are grateful to all of those people and organizations who generously shared their time and expertise.

Cam Birnie

Mike Freese

Darcy Hitchcock

Jeff Israel

Mark Mikolavich

Walt Roberts

Crystal Rutland

Al Siebert

InFocus Corporation

The Pacific Program

# Introduction

Talk with organizational leaders about their most critical challenges and trust is likely to be among the top five. Without trust it is virtually impossible for an organization to achieve the level of focus, commitment, and drive necessary to successfully compete in today's marketplace. Continue the conversation with leaders and you will also find that no two have the same notion of what trust is, much less what it takes to create it. Our objective with this book is to define trust in a way that will help leaders and their employees assess their own levels of trust, and devise strategies for building trust in individual relationships as well as across organizations.

For the past several years we have been researching and experimenting with the concept of trust. We have surveyed an extensive body of literature on the subject and worked with clients to determine the models and tools that best serve organizations in their trust-building work. This book is a compilation of our findings. Along with the models, assessments, and tools for trust, this workbook serves to debunk several misconceptions about trust.

## MYTH: TRUST IS NICE, BUT WE'VE LEARNED TO WORK AROUND IT

Because they haven't a clue how to impact the level of trust in their organizations, most leaders simply try to work around it. The reality is that there is a tremendous cost to low trust. Chapter 1—The Necessity for Trust—details these costs by examining the ways that low trust manifests itself in our lives and business.

## MYTH: TRUST DEPENDS ON THE OTHER PERSON

Talk to people about their low-trust relationships and you will likely hear all that the *other* person has done to damage the relationship. In reality, any failure in a relationship is as much our own responsibility as it is the other person's, and while it may not be to our liking, we've discovered that the most productive place to begin rebuilding those relationships is with ourselves. Chapter 2—The Anatomy of Trust—presents a model for understanding the components of trustworthiness and provides a means for analyzing trust in our relationships.

## MYTH: TRUST EVERYONE OR TRUST NO ONE

Some people assume that there is a "one size fits all" formula for trust; that each relationship should be approached with the same attitude of trust. Our research indicates that this is not only unnecessary, but often unwise. There is for any relationship an "optimal level of trust" in recognition of the fact that some relationships require higher trust than others. Part of this calculation for trust includes determining not only how much is necessary but how much trust is prudent given the context and personalities involved. With this in mind, we also need to be mindful of the assumptions and biases we bring to each relationship and their effect on our ability to build trust where it is called for. Chapter 3—The Willingness to Trust—discusses the concept of optimal trust. It also provides a framework for understanding how our predispositions impact our attitudes for trust.

## MYTH: TRUST TAKES TIME

The time-honored approach to building trust involves waiting and watching. We slowly amass experiences with others as a way of assessing another's trustworthiness. This has become the accepted norm for building trust, but while it has its merits, it is simply too slow a process for our fast-paced world. Organizations are moving at increasing speed making this experienced-based trust building approach untenable. Most organizations need trust now, not in three years. Chapters 4 and 5—The Trust Equation, and Diagnostics for Trust—lay the foundation for expedient trust building. These two chapters provide a model for understanding and testing levels of trust in a variety of relationships so that trust building efforts are focused and directed.

# MYTH: TRUST JUST HAPPENS BY ITSELF

Similar to the "trust takes time" myth is the notion that growth in trust just happens on its own and that we have little influence over the process. This notion excuses our passive approach to building trusting relationships. Nothing could be farther from the truth. In fact passivity in the face of a faltering relationship will do more harm than good. Chapter 6—Developing Trust—outlines six proactive strategies for trust building while Appendix B provides specific structured activities that you can use to forward trust in your own situations.

In addition to debunking the misconceptions about trust, we also hope to build an appreciation for the role that trust plays in an organization's longevity. Our experience in helping organizations transform has taught us that trust is the necessary foundation upon which all progress is built.

Though widely recognized as a key component to healthy productive workplaces, trust is often written off as simply too difficult or ambiguous to deal with. Often a sense of frustration arises in attempting to measure current levels of trust and later, quantifiable progress in building trust. Therefore, Appendix A provides six trust assessments tailored for specific relationships.

Our hope is that this book will not only demystify the concept of trust but provide the strategies, assessments, and tools for consciously and straightforwardly creating trust in your relationships and organizations.

# 1

# The Necessity for Trust

## IS TRUST OPTIONAL?

Success in today's competitive environment demands that organizations be flexible, responsive, quality-focused, relationship-based, and continually innovative. No sector or industry is immune from these demands. They apply equally to public and private, for-profit and not-for-profit, government, quasi-governmental and business, small, large, and multinational alike. Business pundits have loaded us with strategies and models for meeting these demands: total quality management, reengineering, learning organizations, and empowered work teams, to name just a few. Effectively applied, they provide benefits that can mean the difference between being the driver in your industry or the business that is stalled on the side of the road. However, none of them, nor any other improvement effort you try, has any chance of success without a foundation of trust. To ensure a prosperous and lasting transformation it is requisite to first establish a culture of trust. Trust is not an option in the success formula; it is an imperative.

If we dissect the operations of an organization we can see the role that trust plays. We draw upon Scott Sink's model for considering the aspects of an organization from a systems perspective.[1] According to Sink, system performance is comprised of seven critical dimensions:

1. *Effectiveness:* doing the right things

2. *Efficiency:* doing things right

3. *Quality:* delighting the end user

4. *Innovation:* improving continuously

5. *Quality of work life:* providing a safe, inspiring place to work

6. *Productivity:* doing more with less

7. *Profitability:* generating surplus

## Trust and Effectiveness

A client of ours in the biomedical industry had experienced several years of catastrophic performance that undermined trust in the leaders' ability to direct the organization. A culture of blame developed as people began to look for explanations of the failures. Cooperation between product design, production, and quality control disappeared. As a result products got passed around the three departments as many as twelve times before being shipped. In the end, the company had a backlog of orders that kept some customers waiting up to two years for delivery.

While your organization may not be in such dire straits, consider the potential damage of low trust to organizational effectiveness. Employees, customers, and investors have trust in organizations that are perceived to be doing the right thing. This means hiring leaders who appropriately shape their vision and take the right steps to achieve it. Trust is further increased when organizational values align with actions and when there is agreement about what needs to be done. Leaders need a high level of trust in those with whom they share their authority, and employees need a high level of trust in the vision and direction that leaders create for the organization.

Jeffery Pfeffer, professor of organizational behavior at Stanford University, discovered the indispensability of trust. In the book, *Leader to Leader,* he outlines the three basic principles leaders use to transform their organizations: build trust, encourage change, and use appropriate measures of performance.[2] Warren Bennis, one of the most published authors on leadership, concurs that the underlying issue in aligning people with goals and objectives is establishing trust.[3] A study by Royal Dutch Shell pointed to four characteristics common to companies with life spans of 200–700 years:[4]

- They are financially conservative

- They demonstrate sensitivity to the world around them

- They create a sense of cohesion and identity

- They limit central control and exhibit tolerance for activities in the margins

Trust and interdependency are essential to producing the latter two of these characteristics. A sense of cohesion and unity is made possible through a common trust in shared values and purpose. Flatter organizational structures with larger spans of control call for an ownership mentality that can only be derived from a foundation of trust.

Trust creates and sustains a positive environment in which employees feel free to perform and to devote their attention to the goal.[5] A trusting environment permits leadership to implement change strategies and to innovate without encountering resistance from suspicious employees. When each change initiative is met with misgivings and doubt about motives, valuable time and energy are lost. Low trust encourages defensive behaviors. People place filters on their ears and eyes. They only see what reinforces already formed notions. Communications break down and rumors are the primary source of information. At its extreme, lack of trust encourages whistle-blowing or sometimes even sabotage. To ensure effectiveness, then, leaders must instill a climate of trust in order to innovate and transform as the environment dictates.

## Trust and Efficiency

Mistrust creates a breeding ground for inefficiency. Trust is at the root of inspections, checking, and rework. One of our clients determined that 25 percent of professional staff time was wasted redoing work others had already done because of the lack of trust that it had been done right the first time. With hefty average salaries and a professional staff numbering close to 100, this was a staggering direct cost to the organization. High levels of trust, on the other hand, permit reduction in controls, and therefore reduction in costs.

Effective crisis management is also enabled by trust. When there is trust, people collaborate to find solutions rather than searching to put the blame on each other. Another of our clients was facing a dramatic decline in product orders. Making cuts in labor expenses became necessary to keep the company in business. Instead of going behind closed doors to make decisions about who to lay off, the leaders approached the workforce with the situation. Together management and employees came up with creative solutions that saved most people their jobs. Sacrifices were shared (many teams chose to cut everyone's hours rather than risk laying off a member) and cost savings were found in other areas. While the solution was not easy, the company managed to use the unfortunate situation to actually increase trust rather than demoralize the entire workforce.

Solutions, innovations, and improvements are aspects of organizational life that are enhanced by information sharing facilitated by collaboration within a trusting environment. La Porta, Lopez-de-Silanes, Shleifer, and Vishny describe a significant positive correlation between trust and performance.[6] Simply put, trust promotes performance.

## Trust and Quality

Organizations that are sincere in their pursuit of quality know that they must first and foremost earn the trust of their customers in their products and services. As described earlier, trust enables an organization to do things right the first time. But another aspect of our competitive economy requires that we also establish trusting relationships with others outside of our organizations. It is increasingly important to develop trusting relationships with suppliers, customers, and governments, both locally and in the far reaches of the global marketplace. This has become important for several key reasons.

Organizations are forming partnerships with other organizations and putting their futures in mutually dependent relationships. They have come to understand the value of synergistic relationships that cross organizational boundaries. Take for instance the partnerships that major manufacturers have formed with their suppliers. While sole sourcing exposes a business to the potential of disruption, exclusive partnerships also provide the benefit of minimizing variation and reducing costs. To be most effective, however, these partnerships frequently require sharing sensitive product information. Trust enhances the open, direct, and honest discussion needed to make these relationships work. This type of communication helps to reduce the time and cost of negotiation by enhancing the mutual understanding of expectations.

The globalization of the marketplace has put nearly every business in the position of dealing with regulators, customers, or suppliers from cultures alien to our own. Interdependencies are being expanded between differing societies and countries. Presented with so many multiorganizational and multicultural relationships, our old methods of sizing up situations fail us. Our assumptions about who we should trust and who we should not trust are challenged. More than ever we are required to master cross-organizational and cross-cultural relationships. International associations and partnerships demand a close and objective examination of our cultural values and norms. By examining the work we do, we can detect if current approaches are based on some universal truths or on cultural origins. The learning can be enormous, but is predicated on our ability to build trusting relationships with unique and distant people.

Another strategy for competitiveness is benchmarking against other organizations. But benchmarking requires creating relationships with other organizations, other industries, and perhaps even with competitors in order to discover best practices. Trust plays a critical role in developing relationships in which information can be shared in a spirit of cooperation and honesty. The practice becomes a farce if benchmarking information is suspect.

## Trust and Innovation

Shortened product development cycles and an abundance of creative ideas have combined to meet the appetite of a consumer society rich in nonessential buying power. But the faster new products and services are delivered, the higher consumer expectations for newer products and services rise. And the demand does not just apply to business. Citizens are leveraging their power in the voting booth to demand more responsive government. Innovation is being mandated across all sectors: better, faster, and less expensive public services; newer, better consumer products.

Staying ahead of this accelerating demand for innovation requires a lot from an organization. It demands first of all that it continuously generate new ideas. This requires that two conditions be met. First, there must be enough trust within the organization and among its members to enable people to take the risks necessary to admit the status quo is inadequate and to mobilize for change. Second, people need to trust that their ideas will be credited and not used against them. Low trust makes people hold back and test the motives of the organization. Conclusions reached by researcher Horst Kern support this notion. He found that when employees distrust the commitment of their organizations, they fear that innovation might result in job changes or, worse yet, downsizing.[7] Who is likely to step forward with an innovative idea in a culture like this?

Low trust further impedes the innovation process itself. Precious time is often wasted on the monitoring, checking, and supervising encouraged by low trust and suspicion. A flawed innovation cycle which produces many product errors is disastrous to an organization. But a retarded one that is slowed by checks and rework isn't much better. To break open the floodgates of rapid innovation, trust is an imperative.

## Trust and Quality of Work Life

In addition to yielding higher performance, a climate of trust and empowerment taps into the desires of the modern workforce. Ours is a workforce on the move. Having survived the economic shifts of the past four decades, labor has become accustomed to the impermanence of jobs, multiple career tracks, self-branding for the marketplace, and the demise of unquestioned loyalty to a single employer. This modern workforce requires much more than a paycheck or an attractive, cafeteria-style benefits plan. Workers are increasingly expecting to derive meaning, satisfaction, and professional development from their jobs. In order to attract and retain the best and brightest, organizations are compelled to loosen their control to enable empowerment and creativity. A climate of trust is essential for an employer to effectively compete for talent.

Lose trust in the workplace and be guaranteed the loss of a skilled, dedicated workforce. Living in an environment where low trust is the norm creates a state of stress. Watching your back requires enormous energy. Second-guessing the motives of others and having every action you take questioned is a wasteful use of human resources. We yearn for solid, trusting relationships and, over time, will make moves to accommodate this need.

A client of ours, the information technology department of a large transportation company, appreciates this dynamic and has earnestly designed its culture accordingly. Fearful that they could not compete for computer technologists on the basis of salary alone, they purposefully created a highly engaging and empowering work environment and leveraged this aspect of their organization in the quest for talent. Their efforts have paid off; they have the lowest turnover in the Portland metropolitan area though they rank only in the middle in the area's salary range.

## Trust and Productivity

The competitive environment puts unquestionable demands on our workforce. In order to meet the requirements for quality, customer service, and innovation, we need to be willing to unleash the creativity and intelligence of our employees and empower them to solve problems and implement new ideas. An empowered workplace is one that fosters cohesion and cooperation, which result in higher performance and productivity.[8] The payoffs can be very tangible. In 1994, Federal Express and IDS both increased their productivity by up to 40 percent by creating empowered work teams trusted with many of the responsibilities traditionally held by managers.[9] Trust is the key pillar that supports empowerment and cooperation within organizations.

By treating all members of the organization as though they can be trusted, an expectation is formed concerning honest and truthful actions. A paper mill was experiencing theft of its tool supply. Rather than increase security and lock the tools down, they instituted a tool loan program and offered employees the opportunity to borrow tools to do home projects. Not only did tools stop disappearing, but many of the long-missing tools came back. Employees not only behaved in a more trustworthy manner, but they appreciated being treated like responsible adults. When trustworthy behavior becomes a performance requirement, then the people within the organization respond. Likewise, when people are thought *not* to be worthy of trust, it is likely they will live up to that expectation.

## Trust and Profitability

The connection between trust and profitability should by now be apparent. Lack of trust creates expense, wastes time, and causes rework and redundant efforts. It seems that no matter what the presenting organizational problem is, our clients recognize that low trust is frequently at the root. People are crying out for an increased level of trust. Double-checking other's work and questioning motives requires time and energy. And when these precious resources are spent supporting the eroding culture of distrust, the end is in sight. Somewhere in this competitive world, some other organization is not spending its time in this wasteful manner.

A 1999 Watson Wyatt Worldwide survey reported "companies with employees who had high trust and confidence in senior management had a three year total return to shareholders of 108 percent versus a 66 percent return for companies with low trust and confidence levels."[10]

Another research study conducted by The Atlanta Consulting Group, with 395 respondents from 96 different corporations, provides more compelling evidence of the connection between trust and profitability. From this survey they concluded that mistrust is fairly pervasive in our businesses. Only 48% of the people surveyed trusted their bosses and just over half (52%) trusted upper management. While 66% of the respondents admitted that their companies had clearly stated values, only 33% believed they were evident in the actions of the organization. The study further found a high correlation between trust and profitability. In divisions that outperformed others, 84% of survey respondents said they had high levels of trust, as compared to lower-performing divisions in which only 27% believed trust was high. The findings provide evidence of a relationship between the level of trust in organizations and the success of major improvement initiatives like teams, quality, customer services, and reengineering. More importantly, it supports a strong link between trust and overall company results.[11]

When the eyes and attention of the workforce are focused on covering their backs, all of management's pronouncements about an essential goal or competitive initiative are for naught. We may feel good and correct about declaring vital focus areas, but without trust, little will be done to address these areas. The ability to focus externally presupposes that trust exists internally. Trust is an imperative to organizational effectiveness. See Figure 1.1.

**Figure 1.1** Trust's relationship to organizational performance.

# ORGANIZATIONAL CHANGE TO ENSURE LONGEVITY

Without trust, the organization will fail in its requirement to change. But to further emphasize the point, let us draw upon a transformation framework that has been utilized by many to see if trust really is an imperative.

Four essential cornerstones must underlie such organizational transformations as outlined in the book, *Work Miracles*. They are:

- *Self-mastery:* individuals must pursue and achieve personal and professional mastery

- *Interpersonal mastery:* relationships must be managed and nurtured to foster interpersonal growth

- *Value exchange:* the value exchange between parties within the extended system must be clarified and understood

- *Change methodologies:* appropriate methods to drive and enable organizational transformation must be shared and implemented

Together, these four transformation cornerstones provide a framework to continually recreate an organization. Progress is often made on one or two of these cornerstones but the power of integrating efforts to address all four is often overlooked. Developing self-mastery, building interpersonal relationships, creating the sought-after high performance organization, and modeling new tools for change management is demanding. Though difficult, leaders are still called upon to put into place each of the four and do so in an integrated fashion. Addressing all these elements concurrently is demanding.

Now, is trust an indispensable ingredient in executing this model designed for change? Well, it is difficult to see how self-mastery could be achieved without a high degree of trust for self and inner trustworthiness. Obtaining a deep understanding of self requires us to honestly reflect and confront our weaknesses.

Likewise, interpersonal mastery depends upon rapid formation of sustainable relationships. It is hard to envision relationship-building mastery without trust. And forming long lasting value exchanges with customers/suppliers would seem to call upon trust. Finally, the change models we know to be effective rely upon trust as a prerequisite. The models help to create transformation but assume trust is at an acceptable working level. Without trust the transformation cornerstones are ineffective. Transformation is not achieved and the organization eventually dies . . . sometimes overnight and sometimes over a long, frustrating period of time.

## CONCLUSION

Trust is essential in all relationships. Thus, it is imperative to build trust when choosing to work within an organization—an environment of many and varied relationships. The optimal level of trust within each relationship is of our own determination. Having established the need for trust, however, it is imperative to the success of our organizations to be conscious and deliberate about building it.

## KEY CONCEPTS

- Trust is critical to organizational health
- Trust is present within a variety of relationships
- Transforming the organization is needed for survival, and trust is required for transformation

# ENDNOTES:

1. D. S. Sink, W. T. Morris, with C. S. Johnston, *By What Method?* (Norcross, GA: IIE Engineering and Management Press, 1995).
2. J. Pfeffer, "The Real Keys to High Performance," in *Leader to Leader*, F. Hesselbein and P. M. Cohen, eds. (San Francisco: Jossey-Bass, 1999): 279.
3. W. Bennis, *On Becoming a Leader* (New York: Addison-Wesley, 1989).
4. A. de Geus, Sytems in Action Conference, Dutch Shell Study, August 4, 1995.
5. D. M. Daley and M. L. Vasu, "Fostering Organizational Trust in North Carolina: The Pivotal Role of Administrators and Political Leaders," *Administration and Society* 30, no. 1 (1998).
6. R. La Porta, F. Lopez-de-Silanes, A. Shleifer, and R. W. Vishny, "Trust in Large Organizations," *American Economic Review* 87, no. 2 (1997).
7. H. Kern, "Lack of Trust, Surfeit of Trust," in *Trust within and between organizations conceptual issues and empirical applications,* C. Lane and R. Bachmann, eds. (Oxford: Oxford University Press, 1998).
8. P. M. Podsakoff, S. B. MacKenzie, and A. Ahearne, "Moderating Effects of Goal Acceptance on the Relationship between Group Cohesiveness and Productivity," *The Journal of Applied Psychology* 82, no. 6 (1997).
9. B. Dumaine, "The Trouble with Teams," *Fortune* 130, no. 5 (1994): 86.
10. As reported in *Business Ethics Buzz*—business ethics online news June 2000.
11. H. Bracey of the Atlanta Consulting Group

# 2

# The Anatomy of Trust

## WHAT DOES IT MEAN TO BE TRUSTWORTHY?

Think of the person you trust the most. Whether it is your spouse, a parent, grandparent, friend, or a great love, bring that person into your mind's eye. What characteristics and qualities does that person have that inspires such a high level of trust? What does this person have that others do not possess to the same degree? Why do you trust this person the most? Capture your thoughts on paper.

We have posed these questions to many hundreds of people in workshops and leadership forums. Common responses include characteristics like honesty, dependability, reliability, caring, loyalty, concern, truthfulness, shared goals and values, follow through, and support. A picture emerges of a person with high integrity and respect for those he cares about.

Now think of the person who you trust the least. What characteristics and qualities does this person have that cause you to have such a strong level of distrust? As before, write down your thoughts. Answers we've collected to these questions frequently include inconsistency, dishonesty, disloyalty, differing objectives, unreliability, and thoughtlessness. At least those are the printable responses we've seen.

Compare the two lists—the characteristics of the person you trust the most and the characteristics of the one you trust the least. What do you see?

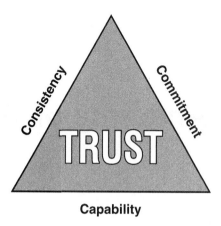

**Capability**

**Figure 2.1**   Trust components—three Cs.

They appear to be polar opposites. In other words the antithesis of the characteristics essential to forming trust are found as the key ingredients in forming distrust. Using this discovery and the data collected from our research surveys and workshop activities, we have identified the three critical components of trust: consistency, commitment, and capability (Figure 2.1).

## Consistency

Consistency is usually the first and most frequently cited attribute that people list in response to our question. There are two aspects to consistency. The first aspect has to do with the match between words and deeds. Does a person live up to their promises and pronouncements? In short, do they "walk the talk." The second aspect has to do with consistency over time. Do they walk the talk every time, all the time? I might follow through on what I say I will do once or even twice, but others want to know that I will be consistent over time before granting me full trust. This is especially important in relationships in which I may not have explicitly stated my intentions. In other words, others may not have heard my "talk." They have only my actions as evidence of my consistencies and will watch to see that my behavior is steady over time. It may be unnecessary to tell you that I value timeliness if I consistently deliver to you on time.

Ross was trying hard to be the empowering supervisor his boss expected him to be, but every time he tried to elicit input from his team he was met with stony silence. Even though he told them over and over that he wanted to hear their ideas, seldom would anyone speak up.

Out of desperation, Ross invited a trusted peer to sit in on his team meeting to provide him some feedback. The meeting was going as usual with Ross doing all the talking. Toward the end of the meeting, one of the team members asked permission to raise an issue. Made bold, perhaps, by the presence of the outsider, he raised an idea that had been on his mind for some time. He proposed changing from a five day, eight hour schedule to four tens. Clearly he had given this a good deal of thought for he began to list the business benefits of his idea. Before he was half-way through his list, however, Ross rolled his eyes and put his hand to his forehead in a "not this again" gesture. He interrupted the team member with "That's out of the question. The union will never go for it." Then he quickly ended the meeting.

Afterward Ross' colleague shared with him what he had observed. It was a classic case of "talking" one thing ("I really want your input") and "walking" another ("I really only want to hear ideas that I like"). Confronted with his inconsistency, Ross was able to understand the mistrust he had created in his team.

Trust grows as our perception of integrity and predictability grow.[1] Captured in this trust element are the attributes of reliability and predictability. Inconsistency erodes our ability to predict another's behavior and puts us perpetually on guard.

In the business environment, not being able to trust the consistency of a supplier or an internal resource is a costly proposition. Redundant systems are put into place to ensure service and these systems come with a price. While building trust does require a good deal of energy itself, the waste, rework, and redundancy associated with distrust far outweigh the investment required to build trust.

We were asked to consult with a government service agency in which a deep and persistent chasm had developed between the local community providers and the state commission authority that supervised them. Solidarity existed on the mission of their efforts, but the actions of the state commission appeared to be out of step with the words of support given to the local service providers. Political positioning and the desire to be on top of current issues put the state commission leadership at odds with being consistent in their actions toward the local communities. What was being declared at a state level was not seen as being produced at the local level.

At first the problem was seen with puzzlement and was assumed to be a simple misunderstanding. Because the inconsistency exhibited by the commission was not addressed, it grew into a major relationship break. The break led to a general distrust between the two parts of the organization, each party accusing the other of having hidden agendas and demonstrating no concern for the agency's clients. The distrust became so great that the once strong link to common commitment was brought into question. Central to our work was shedding light on the inconsistent behavior on both sides. Coming to common agreements about what will happen and how all parties can expect to be treated forms a foundation for holding people accountable to consistent behavior.

## Commitment

There are also two aspects to the attribute of commitment: the concern another is able to demonstrate for us as people and the intention that person has for our common objective. Before we can confidently trust another, we need the assurance that that person has our best interests at heart. We need to know that when the going gets tough, they will stick with us; that they will not abandon us in service of their own self-interest. This kind of commitment is demonstrated through open and honest communication, joint decision making, and consideration of each other's feelings and interests.

The other aspect of commitment deals with the level of commitment another can demonstrate for our common endeavor. Knowing that another is committed to me personally is not sufficient if I am worried that they have no commitment to finishing our project or putting full effort into achieving our goal. We have all probably experienced the awkwardness of trying to work with a dear friend who is not pulling their weight. While we believe they would never intentionally hurt us, we lose trust in their intention to fulfill their obligations.

Paula Shire was an accomplished business leader within her company, InTech. She had served InTech well over the past nine years and had demonstrated loyalty to the corporate vision and collective welfare. As a senior manager in product marketing, she reported directly to the VP of marketing, Carl Zoel. Together they had been working on a complicated and expensive new product introduction. Credibility issues with several product performance claims had emerged. A solution was taking form after much work.

Now it was time to share both the problem and potential solution with the CEO and the executive team. Carl hesitated. When Paula confronted him about his reluctance to expose the problem and forge ahead, Carl shut his office door and began to speak in a direct but hushed voice. He explained that another company had approached him to serve as their CEO. He was going to take the position. His energy to work on the current issues with InTech's new product just wasn't there. Carl's focus was on his upcoming VP position and he said that InTech would muddle through the product issue well enough on their own.

Furthermore, due to his respect for her capabilities and performance, he offered her the position of VP marketing at the new firm. Carl explained that they had always made a strong team and he wanted her to join him in this new adventure.

Paula's belief that the two shared a common commitment to the company was shattered by Carl's comments. Paula could feel the sudden drop in her trust for Carl in the absence of this common, collective commitment. Yes, she was flattered by his comments on her skill level, but his lack of loyalty to InTech was disturbing at best. How could Carl throw off his commitment to InTech so easily . . . in the midst of a company crisis? She had believed that the two of them were in this fight together. But it appeared that Carl was more concerned about his next career move than the performance promises he had made to InTech.

Paula contemplated what her next move should be. Should she continue full disclosure of the project facts to InTech's leadership without support from Carl? Should she confront Carl about his lack of commitment to their employer? Although the job offering was appealing, her sudden drop in trust for Carl made the idea of jumping with him to another company distasteful.

This story demonstrates the dual nature of commitment within a relationship. Commitment is a two-forked proposition. Commitment must be present in two different arenas. First, commitment toward each other as people within the relationship must exist. Believing that another person has your best interests at heart, is supportive of you as an individual, and prepared to back you up in difficult times is one aspect of commitment. But also important in building trust is the shared commitment to a cause or goal. Understanding that common objectives and common value sets exist deepens the relationship. Because you "know how the other person thinks" and their thinking is in line with yours, you can trust their decisions.

Carl did not display the same common commitment to InTech nor the loyalty value that was a part of Paula's makeup. When discovered by Paula, it was a surprise. She had believed their value set and commitment to InTech were in common. The foundation of their relationship was disturbed, and therefore to trust Carl in a new, risky venture seemed out of the question.

The story could have been easily altered to demonstrate the presence of commitment to common value sets and goals, but lack of commitment to the other person. The principle would have shown through equally as well. Both types of commitment are needed to build a resilient trust foundation.

There is, perhaps, no better example of commitment than the story of Malden Mills. In 1995 a fire completely destroyed their Polarfleece manufacturing plant in Massachusetts. The incident presented a prime opportunity for owner Aaron Feuerstein to take the insurance payment and relocate the business to a region where costs were lower, but he chose instead to rebuild in the same community. Further he elected to keep all employees on the payroll in spite of the shutdown the fire caused. This commitment was not one-sided. The employees demonstrated their commitment to the organization by showing up in the midst of the crisis to salvage what they could and clean up what they couldn't.[2]

## Capability

The third component of trust deals with another's ability to produce results or to meet our performance expectations. In other words, does the person have the skills to get the job done? Does this person have the experience or talent to perform well? When an individual or team chooses a lofty goal, trust may be in question when the complexity or requirements of such an accomplishment are not well understood. Assigning people tasks based on their consistency or commitment alone may set everyone up for disappointment if the capability of those people cannot be trusted. This is often the overlooked component of trust; the one we forget when our trust is called into question. Teenagers are quick to challenge a parent's trust in them when denied a request. "Don't you trust me to take the car on this trip?" You might have a very high regard for their consistency and commitment, but they may not have demonstrated their capability as a driver sufficiently to enable you to comfortably toss them the keys to the car.

Mark had performed extremely well as the environmental manager for Chemco. The goodwill produced as a direct consequence of his community work and superior public affairs skills made the firm a national leader. His performance reviews were stellar and he was given maximum merit increases virtually throughout his long career. So when the position of vice president of operations opened up, Mark believed he was in line for the promotion.

However, the president of Chemco, Philip Davis, had not even considered Mark for the position. Yes, he believed that Mark was talented and results-oriented in his current job. On many occasions Philip had lauded Mark's accomplishments in the environmental arena. But Mark had never held an important line position. He had been in support roles his entire career. Making the tough decisions about prioritizing projects, possible staff cuts, or resource allocation were not skills Philip saw in Mark. In fact, he believed that Mark's lobbying for improved environmental performance sometimes ran contrary to optimizing overall economic and operational performance.

When someone else was named VP of operations, Mark was devastated. He simply did not understand why Philip did not trust him to do the job. Hadn't he always been a loyal Chemco manager with exceptional performance? Hadn't he always delivered upon his commitments and demonstrated dedication to results in the environmental area? The plunge toward distrust was drastic. Mark scheduled a meeting with Philip to confront what he considered a lack of support.

Mark was about to be surprised. Philip did trust Mark's commitment to Chemco and to himself as the leader of the company. He did trust Mark's consistency in producing results. But he did not trust Mark's ability to serve as VP of operations. He doubted Mark's capability in such a role, and therefore, did not grant him the position. A superb environmental manager, yes. VP of operations, no. Philip believed the lack of a skill match to the position was obvious.

There is another, even subtler aspect of capability that contributes to the trust formula. That is interpersonal capability. Interpersonal capabilities include the ability to communicate effectively, listen empathically, give honest yet tactful feedback, and manage conflict and disagreements.

Who, after all, would willingly share untested ideas or fears with some-one who does not know how to respond supportively? How eager would we be to confront someone who easily gets defensive? Even if a person has clearly demonstrated technical capabilities, our willingness to extend trust may be compromised if that person doesn't have the skills to be an effective "team player."

Capability represents an often-undistinguished trust element in rela-tionships. Hidden and overshadowed by consistency and commitment, omission of capability in our assessment of others leads to tragic misun-derstandings. Mark believed his boss has an issue with his devotion to Chemco and past performance. When Mark confronted Philip, the potential for the relationship to deteriorate was palpable. Mark's first reaction was to feel betrayed and mistrusted. On the other hand, Philip was surprised. Of course he trusted Mark—in his current position. Philip trusted Mark's con-sistency and his commitment, yes, but not his capability to perform as VP of operations. Unclear about the definition of trust, both contributed to a chasm of misunderstanding.

## ADDING UP TRUST

These three trust elements (the three Cs—consistency, commitment, and capability) form the foundation of trust. All three must be present to create a strong and robust trusting relationship.

Too often we fool ourselves into trusting on the basis of just one or two of these elements. For instance, your judgment of a clearly self-serving per-son—one who has not demonstrated commitment to you or your mutual goal—may be muddled by that person's consistent and capable behavior. Or you may trust a person who you believe to be committed and who has consistently delivered on his word, but who has never demonstrated com-petence at the task you have given them. While business or circumstance may necessitate that we proceed in these situations, we should be careful not to automatically assume our decision translates into unquestioned trust. On the world stage, many a leader has projected strength through capabil-ity and consistency, but any assumption of commitment to the people was made in error. Where trust is given to a leader by people without justifica-tion, disappointment is almost inevitable.

Historian Stephen Ambrose uses General Dwight D. Eisenhower to illustrate a leader's application of the three Cs. With his troops, his staff, his superiors, and ultimately with foreign governments, Eisenhower consis-tently did what he said he was going to do. He had the power of engaging the hearts of his men because of his genuine and evident commitment to

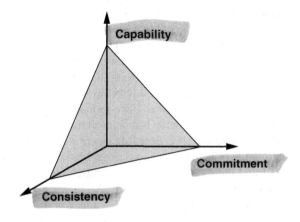

**Figure 2.2** Creating area for trust.

them and their welfare. And unlike General Montgomery, he never eroded trust in his capability by overestimating his own competence. These qualities and skills were rewarded with a high level of trust from those with whom he worked. Because of that trust, and because of the qualities he possessed that brought it about, "he was a brilliant choice as Supreme Commander, Allied Expeditionary Force; quite possibly the best appointment Roosevelt ever made."[3]

As Eisenhower's case illustrates, we can only reliably claim to trust when we are convinced that all three elements are present. The more each trust element is found in abundance, the more the trust capacity expands (see Figure 2.2). It is the area created by our level of confidence in each of the three Cs that expresses the true extent of our trust. If one or two of the trust elements is strong but the third is conspicuously missing, a fully trusting relationship does not exist. Once we thoroughly understand each trust element, the interplay between the elements can be better seen. Seeing the three Cs interact is an important trust analysis skill.

# CLIMATE OF DISTRUST—NEGLECTING THE THREE Cs

Neglecting to build trust can result in distrust. Examining the status of the three Cs helps paint a clearer picture of a company's climate of trust or distrust.

In August 1980, William H. Peace was named general manager of Westinghouse Synthetic Fuels Division, an R&D venture developing a promising coal gasification technology. Peace had to turn the R&D organization into a competitive, profitable business.

For Peace, the mission was about tackling several business issues. He didn't think that people issues would be a major challenge. "After all, if there were such problems, somebody would have told [him] about them."[4]

But distrust had, in fact, reached unbelievable depths. Two managers found the tires of their cars slashed. The morale of line employees was "abysmal." Pranks and hazing were becoming common practice. Cliques of technicians were ruling the shop floor. Managers were afraid of retaliation for taking disciplinary actions. A gap emerged between the long tenured technical staff and the financial/marketing staff recently hired to turn the R&D venture into a business.

How did this organization come to this climate of distrust?

## Substandard Capability

Technicians did not believe finance/marketing people understood the technology and its potential. While at the same time, finance/marketing people thought technicians were ignorant of the requirements for business success.

## Lack of Commitment

Middle management did not demonstrate commitment to the success of the organization when they refused to implement technicians' ideas. Quality circle recommendations were ignored. Technicians believed management's goal was to sell the technology for rapid profit. Management was perceived to have little commitment to the organization and its people. In particular, employees were convinced that Peace was using the division as a stepping-stone to a VP position.

## Inconsistency

The goals of the organization kept changing. Projects were started and stopped. Through small group discussions, management declared their commitment to the people, but they never changed any of their behavior.

Ultimately, Peace created a mutual understanding of the technology and the business requirements, reviewed and reaffirmed the commitment of the management to the organization, and built consistency in the actions of management over time. Through personal introspection, increased communication, and management training, Peace was able to change the organizational climate of distrust to one of trust and eventually achieved his performance goals.

# CONCLUSION

Trust is defined as the presence of three trust elements: *consistency, commitment,* and *capability.* These three Cs are all required to build a bond of trust. However, the existence of a single trust element can lead to the expression of a conditional trusting of that element. Achieving a robust trust in another requires attending specifically to each component. There needs to be an understanding of where consistency stands, where commitment is present, and where capability is required. From this type of analysis a relationship can be strengthened.

Trust is difficult to build or leverage in part because the definition has been so broad and vague. Basing trust on common misconceptions and vague notions undermines the effort. Using the three Cs will help clarify what is present and what is missing in relationships and begin to identify the necessary steps to build or repair trust.

# KEY CONCEPTS

- Trust is the opposite of distrust
- Distrust is costly
- Consistency, commitment, and capability compose the trust elements
- Trust is formed by developing competence in all three of these trust elements

# ENDNOTES

1. D. E. Zand, *The Leadership Triad* (New York: Oxford University Press, 1997).
   R. B. Shaw, *Trust in the Balance* (San Francisco: Jossey-Bass, 1997).
   G. R. Jones and J. M. Georges, "The Experience and Evolution of Trust: Implications for Cooperation and Teamwork," *The Academy of Management Review* 23, no. 3: 1998.
2. L. Prusak and D. Cohen, "How to Invest in Social Capital," *Harvard Business Review* (June 2001): 86–93.
3. S. E. Ambrose, *The Victors* (New York: Touchstone, 1998): 54.
4. W. H. Peace, "I Thought I Knew What Good Management Was," *Harvard Business Review* (March–April 1986).

# 3

# The Willingness to Trust

Developing capacity in the three Cs (consistency, commitment, and capability) is but half of what is needed to build trust. In order to initiate or repair trust in a relationship, at least one player must be willing to take the first step. Willingness is the often overlooked precursor to trust. Perhaps it is because we are so eager to hold others responsible for the low level of trust in our relationships. If we are honest with ourselves, however, we will recognize that we each carry at least half, if not more, of the responsibility for trust.

We are seldom under an obligation to build trust. There is no one keeping score on the number of trusting relationships we have. But if we desire to build trust, our willingness must be established. Even if we are not the initiators, our responses to the overtures of others will determine whether or not trust can grow.

There are three areas in which each of us must test our willingness to move a relationship forward: our willingness, first of all, to *invest the time* and energy it will take to build or repair trust in each relationship; our willingness to *examine the assumptions* we hold which may be blocking trust; and most importantly, our willingness to *take the risk* on which all trust is based. We consider these three factors to be the hinges on the door to trust (see Figure 3.1). Whether you open the door to trust a particular individual or group is a personal choice—no right answer exists. Obtaining a high level of consciousness concerning the degree to which you choose to open the door of trust is the challenge.

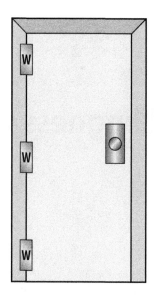

**Figure 3.1** Willingness to open the trust door.

# WILLINGNESS TO INVEST

Building trust requires effort and focus. By clarifying with whom and to what degree you intend to build trust you can increase the speed and likelihood for strong and purposeful relationships. Is it important to build trust with a particular person? While it may seem intuitive, it is surprising how often people enter into a relationship with only a casual intent to build trust. We assume that trust will just happen; that we need only sit back and wait. This approach depends on amassing knowledge of or experience with another person. As we get to "know" someone, our trust gradually grows. While this is a time-honored strategy, it has the distinct disadvantage of taking a lot of time. Waiting and watching is slow, unpredictable, and dependent on serendipity to provide us the right experiences. Given the pace of most workplaces, this option is increasingly untenable.

Being willing to invest in trust asks more of us than patience and passive involvement. It asks us to commit to a conscious and proactive approach in which we are explicit about our intent. Before we make that commitment, however, we must calculate the need for trust and compare it to the investment required to achieve it. This calculation determines the optimal level of trust. We unconsciously engage in this calculation dozens of times a day. Because there is a low level of interdependence with most of the people we encounter in a day, there is a low need for trust and therefore little willingness to invest. We seldom go out of our way to engage the person who picks up our trash or bags our groceries. If we never saw them again, our lives would be little impacted.

As our interdependence with people increases, however, the optimal level for trust increases proportionally. When two or more people's fates are linked, when doing a job requires more than just your own effort, there is a need to develop a trusting relationship in order to efficiently and effectively achieve your common goal. We start to become more aware of the benefits of trust. There is a demonstrated return for investing in the relationship; work will go easier and results are more likely to be better. We decide, sometimes unconsciously, that it is worth our investment of time, resources, and/or energy to build this relationship.

Managers wishing to achieve the gains from a high performance, empowered workforce obviously have a very high need for trust. Empowering employees who you do not trust sets you up for disappointment. Conversely, *pretending* there is trust behind empowerment makes a mockery of employee involvement and undermines management's credibility and integrity. Employees will quickly conclude that empowerment is just another manipulative ploy by management to get more work done for the same pay.

Making the trust calculation more explicit helps us assess the level of effort needed as well as determine the level of effort that is prudent or economical. What level of trust does this relationship call for? What will be the benefit of building trust here? How much effort or expense will it require? What explicitly do I need to do to move forward with trust? It is important to be purposeful in building trust. Conscious effort is what will accelerate the trust process.

One of the issues which often clouds our willingness to trust is the confusion between trust and affection. Somewhere in our unconscious minds we mix the two. Separating them often makes it easier to more accurately assess our willingness to build trust in certain relationships. If we can separate trusting a person from liking a person, we can be more directed in building a relationship that works for our situation. We "like" our spouses, for example, but would not trust them to perform surgery on us. On the other hand, we trust our lives to perfect strangers every time we step on board an airplane. Whether we like the pilots or not has little impact on our trust in their ability to fly the plane. Making this distinction is most important in our work settings where the social aspects of our working relationships blend with the professional need to interrelate.

# WILLINGNESS TO EXAMINE ASSUMPTIONS

Our assumptions about how the world operates form the foundation of our individual beliefs and values. And our beliefs and values are what allow us to make choices and prioritize our lives. They also strongly influence our "predisposition" to trust. In any given situation, our experiences, our culture, and our biases help us determine whether to move forward with trust or withdraw in distrust; whether we approach a situation with a Pollyanna naiveté, a "show me" attitude, or something in between.

Consider how you might react were you to find yourself in either of these two situations.

*Scenario 1*—You are walking down an unfamiliar street shortly after dark. You are alone on the sidewalk except for three approaching figures who are not immediately discernible (Figure 3.2). You are a little nervous as you are not sure how safe this location might be. The three figures turn out to be a young mother dressed in a business suit with her two young children. One of the children is carrying a baseball bat.

*Scenario 2*—You are walking down an unfamiliar street shortly after dark. You are alone on the sidewalk except for three approaching figures who are not immediately discernible (Figure 3.2). You are a little nervous as you are not sure how safe this location might be. The three figures turn out to be three young adult men dressed in low hanging baggy pants, leather jackets, and knit caps pulled low over their heads. One of the young men is carrying a baseball bat.

**Figure 3.2** Willingness to examine assumptions.

What were your reactions to each of the scenarios and how did they compare? What did you find yourself thinking or feeling as you read the two? If your reactions differed, what were the underlying assumptions that led you to the differing conclusions? Did you perceive the baseball bat differently in the two scenarios? If so, why?

There are no right or wrong reactions. But whatever our reactions or responses, they will have influence on the relationships or results of the situation. Each of our responses are colored by assumptions formed by what we were taught (for example, what you may have read in the news about crime statistics), what we have experienced firsthand (perhaps you have been a victim of crime yourself) and by associations we form between new situations and familiar ones (one of the young men may resemble your own son).

Perhaps you consider yourself to be a trusting sort. Maybe you felt no trepidation from either of the scenarios. You can still learn about your assumptions by examining which of two positive perspectives you bring to novel situations. Do you have a general faith in humanity that springs from a belief that people are generally well-meaning and reliable? Or do you strike a trusting stance because you believe that whether people are reliable or not, there is benefit to you in dealing with people as though they were?[1]

By choosing to examine those assumptions you uncover the beliefs that hold truth and those that do not; the beliefs that are working for you and those that are working against you in building trust with others. Noted management consultant and author Peter Block says, "Trust is an expression of our inner world, not a reaction to people and events."[2] He believes that it is far more productive to invert our complaints about lack of trust in someone else and examine how we feel or act when we are with that person. He maintains that it is likely our response to situations that bothers us rather than anything anyone else does. Keeping our feelings and reactions to ourselves enables us to blame the other person for what we are feeling. Our trust is diminished in that person because we gave them the power to affect us. If your goal and intent is to build trust, it may be important to acknowledge and examine the feelings and assumptions that will likely influence your actions. Being aware of the psychological factors at work inside of us can help us challenge nonproductive perceptions.

## WILLINGNESS TO RISK

The most important component in our trust calculation is risk. It's what we measure our investment against, and it's what colors our assumptions and predisposition to trust. While it may be the one thing that most holds us back from pursuing trust, it is by definition necessary to the process. Without risk, no trust is gained.

There are a number of types of risk that play into trust building. When we enter into a trust-building relationship we are putting one or more of them on the line. The risk might be to personal safety, property, existing relationships, or reputation. We put these things at risk in different ways; by exposing our selves (openly sharing proprietary or confidential information; disclosing details about our selves; admitting when we are wrong, sharing our thought processes or our ignorance, and so on), by authorizing others to act on our behalf, by pursuing an untested path/trying something new, or by acting on unspoken agreements. Clearly there are situations where it is imprudent to risk to trust because the cost is too high or because the person or institution in which we are considering bestowing trust has demonstrated untrustworthiness. Most of us exercise what we would call "trust with prudence" which enables us to seek trust even when the payoff is low by minimizing our risk or seeking guarantees to protect our assets.

While we are often acutely aware of what can be lost when we risk to trust, what is often excluded from the calculation is the cost of *not* building trust. Where the risk is too great, we often fall back on contractual arrangements with enforceable consequences. But this protection comes at a cost. The cost is in the controls, the monitoring, the guarantees, securities of deposit, and enforcement. There is also a significant cost in time where trust is low or conditional, the added time and work it takes to double-check, to wait and see. We pretend that conditional trust buys us the time and experience we need to develop the knowledge base for trust. We test each other under controlled conditions first while we check each other out. But this approach may not do what we think. It may only teach us how trustworthy we are under controlled conditions. We each may behave very differently once the controls are removed.

Labor contracts, for example, are designed to protect workers from exploitation. While they are effective at doing this, they also serve to prevent the creation of trust. Relationships may be fine between labor and management in an organization, but there is always the suspicion that it is because of the protection of the contract. No one trusts that the relationship will hold in the absence of a contract. As an example, a paper mill in Oregon was trying to implement self-managing work teams. Everyone (labor and management alike) knew that the old contract system of promoting solely on the basis of seniority was not in alignment with the culture of ownership and empowerment they were trying to create. But as the union steward told us, "when the teams are given the authority to hire, fire, and promote, then we absolutely will do it on the basis of merit. But until management relinquishes that authority, we will continue to do it by seniority." Clearly the union did not yet trust management because they had not yet seen how they would behave in the absence of the guarantees provided by the contract.

Another aspect of risk has to do with the approach we take to it. Do we risk to build trust or do we "risk to disappoint?" Am I really building trust if my risk is to set you up to fail? We've seen this play out many times in organizations. Consider the organization that suffers from low trust between labor and management. Management takes the risk of implementing self-managing teams, trusting team members to make responsible decisions on behalf of the organization. Skeptical of their motives, employees accept the risk of the added accountability but often do so with a risk-to-disappoint attitude. At the first management slip, they triumphantly proclaim the effort is the sham they had suspected all along. Risking to disappoint provides a platform for righteousness and in the end sends trust-building efforts several steps backward.

What if trusting puts more at risk for me than for the other person? What if I've been burned before? How do I know when or how much to risk? We have often been challenged with these questions. Since the choice to risk trust is very personal and situational, there is no right answer. It can be helpful, however, to have a clear understanding of the options. If the inequity in risk disturbs you, consider this—are you sure there is an inequity or is the perception based in your assumptions? Since much of what we put at risk when we trust is intangible (like reputation or relationship), it is very easy to miscalculate what is at stake for both parties. If the risk is quantifiable (like property or money) and is in fact inequitable, then you must still take a step back and calculate the investment you are willing to make. Regardless of what the other party risks, there is still the fundamental question of what you deem the risk to be worth to *you* that may be separate and beyond the other's willingness to invest. Do you want to build trust in this relationship or not?

The conversation is only slightly different when the issue is regaining trust where it has been damaged. We often speculate about the reasons behind the question, "Why should I trust again when I have been burned?" It seems to us that there are four different motivations for the question:

- You simply want the encouragement to do what you know you must do because you still see a payoff to having another go (or else why would you even be considering it?).

- You want help figuring out if you are being unwise. You are unclear about the calculation for trust—how the costs stack up against the benefits.

- You are clear the risk is too great, but still need to move forward with the relationship and don't know how.

- You want someone to agree that you are right about the other person being untrustworthy.

Whatever the motivation you have five different options at your disposal:

1. You can risk again. Only you can decide if this is prudent or wise. Our stance is, however, that trust is not built unless some risk is involved.

2. You can mitigate the risk. You can take another chance, but diminish the possible negative consequences to you. You might trust an employee or team to make purchases, but limit the amount they can spend at one time.

3. You can impose consequences on the other person. This is contractual trust wherein the parties make agreements that link consequences to untrustworthy behavior. If I find out that my team has been using their spending authority for their own self-interests, I can revoke the authority they were given and perhaps impose a penalty or disciplinary action. This approach is often necessary, but it does not build trust.

4. You can back off the relationship. You may decide, after all, that the risk and effort are not worth it. You don't ever have to empower your employees, if you so choose. Clearly, though, no trust is gained if we eliminate the opportunity for building it all together.

5. You can risk to disappoint. I might take a risk knowing that you will fail so that I can righteously break off the relationship. Our litigious society has made this too acceptable an option. We have seen managers set employees up in this way to get the ammunition they need to legally fire them. This is the antithesis to trust building. This approach builds distrust not only with the individual, but also with other employees who witness or hear about your bad faith efforts. And every time you retell the story of your disappointment, you develop additional distrust in others.

# CONCLUSION

Willingness to trust is an often overlooked component of trust, and yet, ironically, it is often the best place to start the trust-building process. Acknowledging the willingness we bring to a relationship is an important first step to progress. It also empowers us with the attitude and clarity we need to move forward with trust. Management consultant Peter Block:

> *I can create a high trust environment anytime I want. All I have to realize is that I am creating the environment in which I live. We are afraid of being naive and a fool if we continue to trust in the face of betrayal. Well, what is so great about being strategic and clever? And what is so wrong about being a fool? Maybe the willingness to be a fool is the exact means of creating the high trust world that we each long for.*[3]

# KEY POINTS

- A first step in the trust-building process involves consciously deciding that trust is necessary and investment must be made to build it

- The assumptions we bring into a relationship can both inhibit or encourage our willingness to trust

- Risk is key to building trust

- With risk, distrust is a possibility

- Risk is greater when the level of trust is unequal or when the consequences of trust are unequal or reciprocity is unequal

- Often we do not take into account the costs of failing to take risks in relationships

# ENDNOTES

1. D. H. McKnight, L. L. Cummings, and N. L. Chervany, "Initial Trust Formation in New Organizational Relationships," *The Academy of Management Review* 23, no. 3 (1998).
2. P. Block, "Trust in Whom," In *News for a Change* (Cincinnati, OH: Association for Quality and Participation, 1998): 11.
3. Ibid.

# 4

# The Trust Equation

## PUTTING IT TOGETHER

We have identified six critical components to trust. The first three—consistency, commitment, and capability—combine to form a definition of trustworthiness. These three attributes are a measure of how deserving a person is of trust; whether someone can be counted on to follow through with their commitments, to keep their word, to stick by others, and to do a job well. The other three components assess one's willingness to enter into trusting relationships with others; the willingness to invest the time and energy, the willingness to examine assumptions and biases, and, most importantly, the willingness to take a risk on someone else (see Figure 4.1).

Taken together these six components form an equation that calculates trust performance (Figure 4.2). The extent to which we can deem ourselves a high performer with regard to trust is a function of our "score" on each of these six attributes.

Clearly, coming up short on any of the six components impacts our ability to form trusting relationships. But it is equally as important to have a balanced score. It is inadequate, in other words, to try to compensate for being untrustworthy by increasing your willingness to trust. Trust performance is a multiplicative function. A zero in either of the two parts of the equation results in a zero product. Based upon the three constructs mentioned previously, a definition of trust is:

*A person's willingness to accept and/or to increase their vulnerability to another person based on their perception of the other person's capability, commitment, and consistency.*

**Figure 4.1**   Trust readiness.

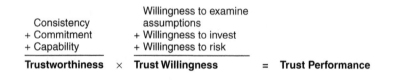

**Figure 4.2**   Trust performance equations.

Picture a person who displays trustworthiness beyond belief, the citadel of the three Cs, but has no willingness to trust. The lack of willingness to invest in trust, examine assumptions, or take a risk would produce few if any trusting relationships. The consequence might possibly be a highly trustworthy loner who is not ready to create meaningful relationships.

On the other end of the spectrum, consider the person who has an enormous amount of energy to form relationships, is open to taking risks, and constantly seeking to understand others. This person is the first to hold out a hand and welcome all. However, unless they can demonstrate some degree of consistency, commitment, and capability, this person is also unlikely to attract anyone into a lasting bond.

# APPLYING THE TRUST PERFORMANCE EQUATION

The trust performance equation helps us understand the components of trust. We are not ready to trust until we have determined both the trustworthiness of the people involved (including ourselves) as well as their willingness to trust. In addition to the components of trust, however, we can approach trust from three different major perspectives or levels: self trust, interpersonal trust, and institutional trust. To better understand these relationships, a model was created to give a holistic view—the trust perspective model.

Building trust inevitably touches on all three levels, but where you begin your trust building work will depend on your situation and your sphere of influence. Always there is work to do on building our own individual capabilities concerning trust, so we put self at the core of the trust perspective model (see Figure 4.3). An organization full of trusting and trustworthy people, however, still may not always ensure an organizational culture of trust. Organizations have their own codes of behavior, rules, and systems that impact the way people interact and determine the behaviors that are fostered. Eventually, if not initially, an organization will need to

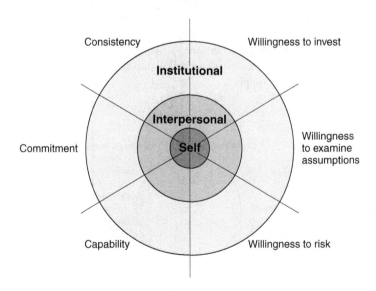

**Figure 4.3**  Trust perspective model.

align its practices to assure that they encourage and support the trusting behavior of individuals. The following sections explain each level in more detail and will help you identify your sphere of concern regarding trust.

## TRUST IN SELF

At the core of all trust work is our own personal relationship with trust. Before we can approach a relationship with anyone else, we must first examine our own trustworthiness as well as our own willingness to trust (see Figure 4.4). The three Cs—consistency, commitment, and capability— help us examine our worthiness as others may perceive it. There may be work we need to do in one or more of those areas in preparation for entering into a trusting relationship with others. Our trust willingness may be tougher to ascertain as it requires us to look deep inside and examine our assumptions, our values, our very beliefs about human nature. We must, in the end, look deep enough to determine the level of trust we have in ourselves. Coming into relationship with self is key to coming into relationship with others.

Focusing on building ourselves to be trustworthy is the primary task. Normally when we begin conversations concerning trust, the direction quickly heads toward what others could do to better build trust. However, the greatest influence we have in building trust with others is first building trustworthiness within ourselves. For once we obtain a high degree of trustworthiness, we will attract others into trusting relationships. Who would want to devote time and energy to a relationship with someone where trustworthiness is in short supply?

**Figure 4.4**   Self and the trust perspective model.

To be considered trustworthy, it is necessary to have demonstrated the traits contained within the three Cs of consistency, commitment, and capability (see Figure 2.2). It is far from sufficient to simply claim proficiency, however. Knowing the skills required to be trustworthy is not synonymous with employing them. Although the spoken word is powerful, eventually people look to see if actions follow.

When contemplating your trustworthiness, another perspective is to measure how you perform in regards to yourself. In other words, do you keep agreements with yourself? What is your commitment to yourself? Are you knowledgeable and frank about your capabilities to yourself? Your skill in building external trustworthiness is dependent upon building trust with yourself. The question has been asked many ways in the past, "Are you your own best friend?"

Imagine a loved one, friend, or co-worker giving a testimonial in your behalf with respect to your trusting nature, readiness, and fitness in producing trusting relationships. Envision your reputation for trust integrity as extremely high and that you have built lasting and profoundly strong relationships. Possibly the tribute might sound like this:

You can always count on Ray to deliver what he promises. He comes through for you. At first I was a little confused by his exactness in understanding the nature of any agreement we were discussing, be it the time and place for a lunch or something of great financial concern. But I began to realize that Ray does this to make sure he understands and is prepared to fulfill any agreement he makes. And meet agreements he does. His word is truly his bond. The few times something goes astray or is partially done, Ray is the first to acknowledge the breakdown and moves to make it right. He seeks you out to fix the agreement, and deliver on the original intent.

But it is more than just keeping promises. He displays a genuine commitment to others. He listens intently and devotes his attention to really understanding. By no means do we always agree, but I believe Ray could represent my thoughts better than I could . . . even when he has the opposite opinion.

I also appreciate the risks he has taken with me. And because he is so committed, I feel obliged to be the same. This has forged a real trusting relationship. I value his openness, his truthfulness, his honesty and most of all his friendship. He is the most trustworthy guy I know.

Think about having such words said about you. See yourself in your mind's eye as the epitome of a trustworthy and trust-willing person. What would be necessary for you to do in order to close the gap between this ideal and your current performance in building such relationships? Can you see where improvement is called upon?

Now you have a place to begin work in becoming trustworthy and trust willing. A self-assessment concerning individual trustworthiness can be found in Appendix A. The assessment serves as a reflective guide and aids in identifying personal performance gaps. When coupled with feedback from others with regards to our individual trustworthiness, it can be a beneficial tool.

# INTERPERSONAL TRUST

The most common trust perspective deals with trust between people. We distinguish between two kinds of interpersonal trust: the trust between you and one other person and the trust relationship that exists among members of a team of interdependent people (Figure 4.5). While many of the issues are the same, there are some subtle differences that affect the trust-building process.

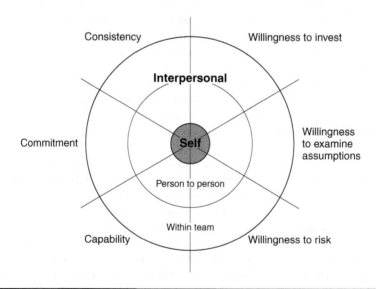

**Figure 4.5**  Trust perspective model—adding interpersonal.

## Person to Person

Building trust between two people is an intimate process that is based mostly on the participating parties' willingness and ability to engage in honest dialogue. At some point the conversation must turn to a mutual assessment of the level of trust each feels for the other and the basis for that assessment. The diagnostic tools that are included in Appendix A should enable you to facilitate a pointed and constructive conversation about where you feel the other person earns your trust and where you believe attention needs to be paid in order to foster additional trust. Since the diagnostics use specific behavioral descriptors to dissect trust in the relationship, you can use the assessment items to describe the behaviors and interactions you would like to see. Focusing the conversation on what you can and should do is a much more constructive approach than complaining about what another person isn't doing. The hardest part of the dialogue, but perhaps the most productive, will be identifying what each of you is willing to risk in order to further the relationship.

## Within Teams

Building trust within a team requires a slightly different approach because individuals have a different relationship with teams than they do with other individuals. Taking risks, for example, is often easier for people to do in groups because we feel protection in numbers. Sorting out the complexity of the myriad of interrelationships among the various members of a team, however, can confuse the issue of trust. The best place to start with building team trust, then, is with the processes used to create the team.

Consider first of all whether you have the right members on the team. We don't just mean people who get along well together, but people who have the skills to fulfill the team's mission. Selecting team members for the contribution they can make and then assigning roles and responsibilities in such a way that leverages those talents builds the team's capability. Since it is not always easy to make appropriate assignments, ensure that the team has a process for rotating assignments, supporting each person in his or her role and developing competency to assure that inappropriate assignments do not erode trust and performance.

It is also helpful to facilitate a conversation among team members about what they hope to achieve as a group and what each individual wants to achieve for him or herself. Conversations of this sort help build commitment among team members. It is difficult to commit to anything over which we feel no influence, so ensure that participation in these conversations is balanced and that a consensus process encourages full support for ideas and decisions.

Lastly, team members should come to explicit agreements about how they want to work together and how they expect to be treated on the team. This should also include designing processes for holding each other accountable for individual and collective responsibilities. Having this conversation early—before any conflict may arise—makes it easier to handle difficult or unexpected situations when they do arise. It also supports consistent behavior among members as well as from the team as a whole. These conversations may also reveal personal assumptions or concerns that may be getting in the way of trust development.

Once the team is up and running, there are some habits it should develop to keep trust building. The team should be disciplined about providing feedback to members on how they are doing—including recognition for work well done, suggestions for how to contribute better to the team, and reminders of expectations and commitments. The team should also make time to play—allowing team members to get to know each other personally to strengthen the bond among them, and to pay attention to the individual members' needs for support.

# INSTITUTIONAL TRUST

The third perspective, institutional trust, looks at an organization as its own entity. While often difficult to pinpoint, nearly every employee has a "gut feeling" about the culture of trust (or distrust) in their organization. Most could give a fairly accurate assessment of how trustworthy the organization is; how willing it is to invest in trust, check the deeply embedded cultural assumptions on which it operates, or take risks as an organization. As indicated in our diagram (Figure 4.6), you can see this aspect of trust play out in the relationships between teams or departments in an organization. You can also see it in the organizational culture that crosses and infects all parts of the organization and is the basis for its policies, procedures, and business systems. It is further reflected in the relationships an organization creates with others outside of its boundaries.

## Team to Team

While trust between teams or departments is strongly influenced by the trusting culture of the organization as a whole, there are several contributors to distrust that play out specifically at this level.

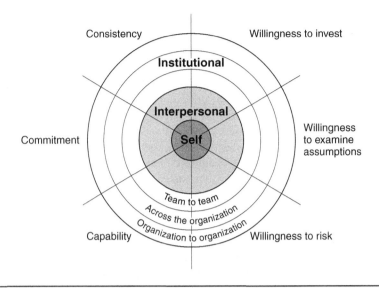

**Figure 4.6** Trust perspective model—adding institutional.

**Conflicting priorities.** In one of our client organizations trust had broken down between two departments in the manufacturing facility. The dispute arose between the process engineering group, whose job it was to design and document the manufacturing processes, and the facilities maintenance team, who was responsible for keeping the plant up and running on a daily basis. While on the surface it seemed that they shared a common goal (effective and efficient operation of the plant), in practice they often found that their priorities were at odds. The engineers' performance was measured by the long-term operational costs of the plant so their focus was on system-wide optimization. The maintenance crew's success, on the other hand, depended on minimal equipment downtime. Quick fixes took precedence over long-term solutions because they were less disruptive to production. Where you have teams or departments that seem to be at odds, begin by first identifying their respective accountabilities to see if they are in conflict.

**Competition for resources.** You can also predict that trust between teams or departments will erode if they feel they are competing with each other for resources. Competition can be insidious within an organization. It is nearly impossible to feel trust for those with whom you are competing as they can only be relied upon to look out for themselves. Eliminating this competition, whether perceived or real, will level the playing field and allow the teams to begin a constructive dialogue about trust.

**Confusing reporting structures.** Unclear reporting responsibilities erodes both commitment and consistency. In a large manufacturing organization we recognized that the source of conflict between the production department and the quality assurance department was rooted in a confusion as to whom each department was accountable. The QA department felt it was their job to represent the needs of the customer. As a result, they established very high standards for production and rejected product that didn't meet those standards. Production felt that QA should have been accountable to helping them develop processes that met standards the first time instead of increasing their costs and delays by repeatedly rejecting product. QA lost trust in production's capability to consistently produce quality product; production lost trust in QA's commitment to them and the goals of the production department.

## Across the Organization

The next ring on our model encompasses the organization as a whole and we find that the farther from the individual we move, the more complex the issue of trust becomes. When examining the culture of trust in an organization we find that there are two places you can intervene to impact institutional trust: leadership and organizational architecture.

**Leadership.** Does trust in leadership really make any difference? Or is trust simply an environmental condition, existing at differing levels, apart from a performance influence? Kurt Dirks conducted an empirical study examining the relationships among trust, leadership, and team performance. He wanted to test the widely held assumption that a team's trust in its leader has a significant effect on the team's performance. His study focused on the performance and results of NCAA basketball teams. He discovered evidence indicating that trust in leadership is both a product and a determinant of team performance. In other words, leadership produced superior results when a high level of trust existed, and when positive performance was present, an increased level of trust was consequential.[1]

How do leaders develop trust? They must first of all deliver results. An unsuccessful organization is a breeding ground for cynicism and insecurity. Leaders who can't deliver results have no credibility with employees and inevitably appear either two-faced or incompetent. Leaders must also operate with integrity. This means making their values clear and then behaving in alignment with them. It also means keeping commitments, admitting when they are wrong, and using the mistakes of others to foster learning rather than retribution. Further, leaders must demonstrate concern for all members of the organization. And it has to be genuine concern. Employees can spot a fake from a mile off.

Finally, leaders need to demonstrate and extend trust. Leaders that display trust create an environment in which people are more likely to trust one another. By contrast, when managers display distrust, they subtly encourage others to do so as well.[2]

In their book, *Lesson from the Top,* Thomas Neff and James Citrin studied 50 top leaders, from Jack Welch at General Electric to Andy Grove at Intel. A common commitment by all 50 leaders to "doing the right things right" was a key finding. The authors go further to describe this commitment as a focus on living in integrity and leading by example.[3] Living in integrity draws people into relationships of integrity, relationships built upon openness resulting in a high level of trust for the leader. Leading by example requires consistency between the walk and the talk. And choosing the right things and being able to accomplish these objectives displays a capability. No wonder these top leaders develop deep trusting relationships with associates, suppliers, and customers.

**Organizational architecture.** In addition to strong leadership, organizations need the architecture (the systems and structure) to foster trust. Robert Shaw, in his book *Trust in the Balance*, identifies the critical strategies for developing an architecture of trust.[4] The basis for such an architecture is a clear vision and aggressive but achievable goals. Without an inspiring vision and clear direction, employees are unlikely to commit their energies or faith. Accountability is another important component. Though many leaders think it benevolent to protect their employees from real consequences, in fact they do them and the organization a grave disservice. People trust more when accountabilities are clear and consistently enforced.

Another aspect of organizational architecture is the information systems that control the flow and accessibility of information. Organizations that restrict access to information through hierarchical flows, security blocks, filters, or closed meetings, create an environment of suspicion. Sharing information openly, on the other hand, demonstrates both commitment and a willingness to risk for trust.

As we have said before, a management philosophy based on empowerment builds trust within an organization as well. Authorizing people to make decisions on behalf of the organization demonstrates trust and is more frequently rewarded with trustworthy behavior. Empowerment is further bolstered by feedback and recognition systems that reward collaboration, open sharing, and measured risk taking.

## Organization to Organization

More and more organizations are finding it important to develop relationships with other organizations in order to further their objectives. For example many organizations have learned that it is better to work with rather than against labor unions. Similarly, the quality movement made a good case for sole-sourcing materials from trusted suppliers to assure consistent quality as well as good price. Reengineering led some organizations to partner with specialists and outsource non–core functions or services. Developing workable relationships with local government and community groups helps organizations maintain a skilled labor supply as well as favorable tax and zoning arrangements. For some organizations, partnering with environmental or special interest groups is necessary to maintaining a good reputation in the marketplace. And mergers and acquisitions present a whole new set of relationship challenges. British Telecom learned through its failed attempt to merge with MCI that "trust, understanding, and equity are as important as strategic, technical, and financial issues."[5]

These organization-to-organization relationships are especially complex because they rest on dozens of key interactions among various and sometimes changing members of the respective organizations. Depending on the nature of the relationship you are trying to build, you may find that you are involving people from very disparate parts of the participating organizations: purchasing, engineering, manufacturing, quality, sales, environmental, human resources, accounting, legal, in addition to the executives and other high-level managers involved in initiating or directing negotiations. Further complicating this trust perspective is the influence of any perception of inequity between the participants. Suppliers often feel disadvantaged in a relationship with their customers. Similarly, unions and environmental groups may feel outpowered by corporate strength. Research suggests that when one party believes that equity is lacking, skepticism will likely hinder the trust-building process. Special consideration should be allotted to the more vulnerable party in order to proceed with trust.

While the complexity of these situations belies the possibility of a simple solution, we have identified a process for at least initiating trust building between organizations.

1. *Assess the need for trust.* The first step is to assess the need for trust. Since each situation will be different, the need for trust will vary accordingly. The one axiom that applies across all situations is the idea that the higher the level of interdependence among the parties involved, the higher the need for trust. Where a customer, for example, has many choices for suppliers, the need for trust is lower than in relationships where an organization is seeking to develop a sole-source relationship for materials.

2. *Assess the level of trust.* Assuming there is a recognized need to develop trust, the next step is for the trust-initiating organization to take a careful assessment of its own trust readiness. And since there may be multiple employees who will represent the organization in this relationship, it is important that all stakeholders participate in the examination of trust readiness as a group.

3. *Declare your intentions.* The third step is to declare your intent to build trust with the other organization. This involves presenting your understanding of the benefits of a trusting relationship as well as your assessment of the effort and actions needed to achieve it. As initiator of the process you have a special obligation to be honest, open, and direct about what you want. This requires openly sharing your insights and learning from your self-assessment process. The honesty and candor with which this presentation is done will enable the process to proceed to step four.

4. *Help your partner self-assess.* Step four involves engaging the partner in their own self-assessment of their trust readiness.

5. *Exchange feedback.* The last step requires the participating organizations to exchange constructive but candid feedback about each other's performance and to share their expectations for what will change with each other.

This process sets the stage for trust. To assure that it will flourish, the participating organizations should build a supporting communication infrastructure so that information and feedback flow efficiently and directly to the appropriate parties. Regular check-ins will also help keep efforts on track and minimize unexpected events or actions.

# CONCLUSION

In addition to understanding the components of trust, it is useful to identify the different places where trust is both low or high within an organization. Though every level of perspective on trust is based on both trustworthiness (consistency, commitment, and capability) as well as trust willingness (willingness to invest, examine assumptions, and risk), each level, or perspective, of trust implies a different approach and different considerations. Repairing or building trust at just one level may be insufficient to create a full culture of trust within an organization. Use the model to determine your area of need or the best point to intervene to develop trust within your organization or key relationships. The next chapter introduces assessments linked to each level that will further dissect and diagnose trust.

# KEY POINTS

- Trust readiness is a function of each party's trustworthiness and trust willingness

- Trust can be approached from any one of six perspectives: self trust, person-to-person trust, trust within teams, trust between departments or teams, an organization's culture of trust, and trust between organizations

- While the trust readiness of individuals is critical to achieving a culture of trust in an organization, so too is it important that the organization's systems, policies, norms, and practices align with values of trust

- Leaders play an important role in influencing the culture of trust in an organization by modeling trustworthy behavior and by filling leadership positions with trustworthy people

# ENDNOTES:

1. K. T. Dirks, "Trust in Leadership and Team Performance: Evidence from NCAA Basketball," *Journal of Applied Psychology* 85, no. 6 (2000): 1004–1012.
2. L. Prusak and D. Cohen, "How to Invest in Social Capital," *Harvard Business Review* (June 2001): 86–93.
3. T. J. Neff and J. M. Citrin, *Lessons from the Top* (New York: Pengin Books, 2000).
4. R. Shaw, *Trust in the Balance* (San Francisco: Jossey-Bass, 1997).
5. Prusak and Cohen.

# 5

# Diagnostics for Trust

The previous chapters provide a grounding in the concepts of trust. This chapter introduces a set of assessments that translate those concepts into specific behaviors and practices for the purpose of diagnosing the level of trust in your own relationships. This assessment process will enable you to focus your trust-building efforts on those areas where they will have the most impact.

There are six assessments provided in Appendix A of this book. Each of the assessments maps to one of the three levels in our trust perspective model: self, interpersonal, and institutional. The three Cs (capability, consistency, and commitment) and three Ws (willingness to invest, willingness to examine assumptions, and willingness to risk) form the pillars of each assessment (see Figure 5.1). A separate assessment was designed for each level so that you would have a diagnostic tool to address the specific relationship of concern to you. The three sections that follow describe the focus of each assessment.

## SELF ASSESSMENT

At the core of all trust work is personal mastery. We put it at the center of our model to illustrate that all work with trust emanates from our own ability to both project and attract trust. We encourage everyone to begin by taking the Self assessment because personal mastery is a prerequisite to healthy relationships at all levels of an organization. Use this assessment to identify your own level of trustworthiness and trust readiness.

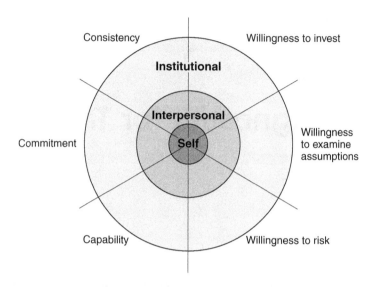

**Figure 5.1** Trust perspective model.

Taking the time to reflect upon our trustworthiness is valuable. But if not done in concert with feedback, we can lose touch with reality. If truth has its roots in our accumulated assumptions about how things are, then using only our viewpoint could lead to a distorted reality. Bring in the gallery. How do others see you? Do they see you as consistent, dependable, and delivering upon your agreements? Do they see you as a person of conscious commitments, committed to others as well as to a shared vision? Do they see you as knowledgeable of your capabilities, not underplaying your skills or exaggerating your abilities? These are the types of questions that can add light to our understanding of our trustworthiness.

Asking others about our trustworthiness can be humbling, especially when we request feedback from a broad selection of people. But is there some hidden benefit to asking for feedback in itself? When given the task of seeking feedback from others, workshop participants invariably report an increase in trust within the relationship by virtue of initiating the conversation. We have seen even the most caustic relationship improve when one party requests trustworthiness feedback. And we have seen strong relationships become more robust as a result of requesting feedback. We recommend asking many for input. The benefits are twofold: you can gain valuable knowledge regarding how you are viewed and you can actually build trust in the process.

# INTERPERSONAL ASSESSMENTS

Usually when we think about trust it is with a particular relationship in mind. While it is important for each of us to develop our individual capacity for trust, it is not until we enter relationships with others that this capacity is tested. We have identified two levels of interpersonal trust: the relationships we create with individuals and the special relationship that results among a group of interdependent team members. Use the Person to Person assessment if your aim is to develop or mend relationships with individuals. The Within Teams assessment is useful if your concern is with trust among team members. This assessment will help a team to identify the culture of trust present and the behaviors that either contribute to or undermine trust.

# INSTITUTIONAL ASSESSMENTS

As relationships expand to include more people, it can become harder to understand how to intervene to build trust. The last three assessments deal with measuring trust at these larger scales. The Team to Team assessment focuses on the relationships that cross teams or departments. Depending on the structure of an organization, functions or operations can become fractured, creating impermeable walls between groups that need to work together. If this is your focus of concern, use this assessment to identify what trust (or its absence) looks like at this scale. This assessment is particularly useful when relationships between teams or functions (for example between engineering and production, or accounting and purchasing, and so on) have broken down.

The organizational assessment looks at the organization as a whole. It measures the behaviors of an organization's leaders and systems to determine the "culture of trust" present. This assessment can help you determine the perception employees have of the organization while at the same time clarifying what trust looks like at this level. If you choose to address trust at this level, you may want to administer this assessment with all employees or with a representative sampling of employees. As with any employee survey, you should be prepared to share data and resulting decisions or actions in a timely manner.

The last assessment, Organization to Organization, is useful to those businesses that want to create a trusting relationship with entities outside of the organization. These might include vendors with whom it is beneficial to develop a close partnering relationship, unions in order to facilitate negotiations, or nongovernmental organizations (NGOs) or regulatory agencies to maintain a positive public image. It is recommended that all the relevant stakeholder organizations participate in this assessment process.

# ASSESSING THE COMPONENTS OF TRUST

Though each of the assessments focuses on a different level of relationship, all six assessments in Appendix A follow the same format and organization. There are three parts to each of the six assessments. Part One asks respondents to assess the overall level of trust, Part Two assesses each of the six components of trust, and Part Three provides a score sheet for calculating a trust score as well as suggestions for tools or strategies for building trust.

### Part One—Overall Assessment

Each diagnostic begins by asking the respondent to estimate both a current overall level of trust for the targeted relationship as well as an estimate of what they believe the level should be to meet needs or expectations. The scale used to measure the level of trust goes from extreme distrust to very high trust. The middle of the scale indicates a neutral level. The samples that follow are from the interpersonal assessment titled Person to Person.

---

## TRUST ASSESSMENT

## PERSON TO PERSON

This questionnaire is designed to help you build trust in a relationship with one particular person. There are two parts to this assessment. The first part asks you to take a quick overall measure of your level of trust with your chosen person. The second part dissects trust into its six component parts and helps you assess where your relationship is strongest and weakest.

### PART ONE: OVERALL ASSESSMENT

On a scale of 1–7, how would you rate your current level of trust with this person?

| Strong Mistrust | 1 | 2 | 3 | Neutral 4 | 5 | 6 | 7 | High Trust |
|---|---|---|---|---|---|---|---|---|

On a scale of 1–7, what level would you like your trust with this person to be?

| Strong Mistrust | 1 | 2 | 3 | Neutral 4 | 5 | 6 | 7 | High Trust |
|---|---|---|---|---|---|---|---|---|

---

The purpose of this initial assessment is twofold. First it establishes a benchmark or a "score" that defines trust for the respondent. Secondly it makes explicit, and to some extent measurable, the gap between the current state and the desired or needed state. This step is important to establish a willingness to invest in the relationship.

## Part Two—The Components of Trust

The second part of each assessment measures the six components of trust: the three Cs—consistency, capability, and commitment, and the three Ws—willingness to invest, willingness to examine assumptions, and willingness to risk. Each component is defined by a set of behaviors or practices that are presented in opposing pairs. Respondents are asked to consider which of the extreme descriptions in each pair their relationship most resembles. They have the option of selecting a value that matches one or the other description, or indicating the extent to which their relationship more or less resembles one of the descriptors. One of each pair of behaviors describes actions which build mistrust while the other describes behaviors that build trust. The scale between the descriptors matches the 1–7 scale used in Part One so that the respondent can either validate or correct their initial overall assessment.

The behaviors or practices that make up the assessment items serve several purposes. They help to further define each of the components of trust while at the same time provide specific, observable actions that lend some validity to the respondent's assessment of trust. They also suggest actions participants might begin to employ to improve the level of trust. The sample below shows the first seven items taken from the Person to Person assessment.

---

### PART TWO: TRUST COMPONENT ASSESSMENT

The following questions will help you identify the domains in which your trust is strongest and weakest. The contrasting descriptions are designed to provoke your thinking regarding trust. For each row, indicate the point on the continuum (from 1 to 7) that best describes this relationship. A "1" indicates that the description on the left describes the relationship perfectly. A "7" means that you match the description on the right. If neither provides a perfect description, use the rest of the scale to indicate where between the two extremes you think you fall. Circle your answers and calculate your totals for each element of trust.

---

| **Capability** | | | | | | | | |
|---|---|---|---|---|---|---|---|---|
| 1. We hide our shortcomings from each other. | 1 | 2 | 3 | 4 | 5 | 6 | 7 | We are honest with each other about what each of us can and cannot do. |
| 2. We lack the skills it will take to fulfill our obligations to each other. | 1 | 2 | 3 | 4 | 5 | 6 | 7 | We both have the technical skills we need to fulfill our obligations. |
| 3. We have no solid knowledge of each other's competence. | 1 | 2 | 3 | 4 | 5 | 6 | 7 | We have clearly demonstrated our competence to each other. |
| 4. We seldom hear what the other is saying. | 1 | 2 | 3 | 4 | 5 | 6 | 7 | We listen empathically to each other. |
| 5. We do just enough to get by. | 1 | 2 | 3 | 4 | 5 | 6 | 7 | We both work to be our best. |
| 6. We seldom provide each other feedback and when we do it is confusing or hurtful. | 1 | 2 | 3 | 4 | 5 | 6 | 7 | We frequently give each other pointed and helpful feedback. |
| **Total Score:** | | | | | | | | |

Respondents are instructed to total the values of each of the numbers they circled in the six component sections. These numbers are then transferred to the score sheet in Part Three of the diagnostic.

## Part Three—Assessing the Results

Part Three includes instructions for calculating the trust score. Respondents are asked to transfer their total scores for each of the six components to the appropriate box in the scoring worksheet. Each component total is then divided by the number of items in that section to obtain an average component score on a 1–7 scale. This calculation will enable the respondent to pinpoint where trust is both strong and weak.

## PART THREE: ASSESSING THE RESULTS

Enter your total score for each section in the score column and multiply it by the factor provided. You will obtain a "score" that matches our 1–7 scale. Then total the three scores in each section and multiply by the factor provided to get a score for both trustworthiness and willingness to trust.

| | Score | # of Items | Result |
|---|---|---|---|
| Capability | | ÷ 6 | |
| Commitment | | ÷ 7 | |
| Consistency | | ÷ 5 | |
| **Trustworthiness** | | ÷ 18 | |
| Willingness to invest | | ÷ 3 | |
| Willingness to examine assumptions | | ÷ 6 | |
| Willingness to risk | | ÷ 7 | |
| **Trust Willingness** | | ÷ 16 | |

Compare your calculated component score with your initial overall assessment in Part One. Does your calculated component score match your initial estimate of the current level of trust? How large is the gap between the calculated score and the level of trust you want to have? Use the component scores and the suggested tools to design a strategy for building trust.

Each assessment concludes with a list of tools from Appendix B that can help build trust for the particular level of relationship. The list is a suggested menu from which to select. It is not an ordered or sequenced list of prescribed activities. Choose from among the list the tool or tools which best suit your situation.

## Tool Suggestions

Consider using the following tools to help you build your trust capacity:

- Key relationship and trust
- Dialogue
- Ladder of inference
- Left hand column
- Purpose hierarchy
- Interface conflict solving model

# CONCLUSION

While our models help people understand what trust is about, the assessments help them prepare for the work of building or repairing trust. By describing specific behaviors, people are able to see where trust is being damaged and what it will take to remedy it. Once you have identified your area or relationship of concern (relationship with another person, among team members, between teams, within an organization or between organizations) you can use the corresponding assessment to better understand the relationship and begin the journey towards trust. Careful administration of these assessments is a critical first step to the work of consciously and capably building trust.

# KEY POINTS

- Take the Self assessment no matter where you feel trust is a problem in your organization

- Use the assessments not to "rate" your relationship, team, or organization, but to identify opportunities and strategies for improving trust

- If you choose to address trust in groups or in an organization, protect the anonymity of respondents

- If you are assessing more than one other person, be sure to follow up with results and engage participants in a dialogue about what they would like to do

# 6

# Developing Trust

## DEVELOPING TRUST

So far, we have covered trust from definition and analysis points of view, as well as provided tools for assessing trust from six different perspectives. In this chapter, we present several considerations for approaching trust development. What we have learned is that the knowledge of trust is of little value in the absence of deliberate action. Our interest as authors is to have relationships prosper across organizations due to the application of our findings and strategies. It would be a disservice to these writings if intellectual musings were the sole outcome of reading the text. Worse would be to learn the tools of trust and use them as "weapons" against others who we deem need "fixing." This would miss the point that the source for trust building lies within ourselves.

We are calling upon outlays of energy for the express purpose of creating trust in targeted relationships. By "targeted relationships" we mean those relationships where both the need and desire for trust is great enough to justify the investment of time, focus, and spirit. We present here strategies for developing trust that fall into the three critical focus areas identified in our trust perspective model: self, interpersonal, and institutional. Appendix B contains specific activities and processes which can be used to support these strategies.

## DEVELOPING SELF

Where development of personal trust performance is the goal, we prescribe two strategies for developing self: look inside (take a self-assessment, and make plans for improving your trust readiness), and determine direction (understand who you are and where you are going; determine your life's purpose). When these two actions are taken, a strong, attracting magnet of trust is developed in self. Self-confidence grows, confidence grounded in self-awareness and purposefulness.

## Look Inside

Trust building is a passage, a series of actions that, over time, have the potential to create thriving relationships. As we have explained, developing trustworthiness in self is the critical first step. It is hard to imagine having trusting relationships when significant trust flaws exist in self. A truthful examination of self will reveal the most powerful leverage points for moving trust forward. As you conduct your self-assessment, consider three aspects of your conduct: your trust with yourself, your trust for others, and your trustworthiness (Figure 6.1).

It is useful to begin a self-examination by testing trust for self. When commitments are made to self, about self, do we follow up? Are commitments made at all with self, or do you avoid that risk altogether? The three Cs and three Ws apply to our relationship with self as well as with others. Without being a trusted friend to yourself, the corrosive power of distrust has already been activated. When you are unable to keep a promise to yourself, the pattern has been laid for your relationships with others. Visualize a conversation with yourself. What do you hide from yourself? Where are you not truthful or consistent? Where do you under- or overestimate your own capability? Listen to your own inner dialogue as you set goals or plan your day. Take an honest look inside.

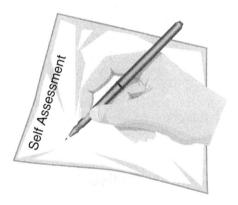

**Figure 6.1**   You assessing you.

Next take a candid assessment of your predisposition to extend trust to others. Review the three Ws—willingness to invest in others; willingness to expose your assumptions, biases, and blind spots; and willingness to take risks in relationships. What are the criteria you use to decide whether trust is important or necessary in a relationship? How thoroughly do you examine the notions or expectations you consciously or unconsciously bring to a relationship? How much are you willing to risk? What limits do you put on risk and how much of those limits are carried over from other relationships or experiences? We are often too quick to blame others for low trust without first admitting to the barriers we may contribute ourselves.

Finally, take an honest look at your behavior in relationships. How do you rate on the three Cs (consistency, commitment, and capability)? When we become trustworthy, we tend to attract people with the same values. The principle of social proof reveals our propensity to imitate others.[1] We tend to look first to see what others are doing or saying before doing or saying anything ourselves. In other words, human beings are prone to conformity. By behaving in a trustworthy way, we cause others around us to act the same. By stepping out for trust, we influence people throughout society.

Let's see how your being trustworthy plays to a bigger audience. Imagine pointing out to a convenience store clerk that you've been given too much change. The mistake is obvious to you, but the clerk has made the error and is already moving to the next in line. Picture the others in line seeing the transaction. As you call attention to the overpayment, the others in line observe a cultural display of honesty. The residuals from honest and trustworthy behavior continue to be experienced beyond the actual exchange. An expectation of correct payment for purchases is created . . . no walking off or coming up short by either side. The air of commercial honesty is enhanced, and this bias towards honesty will have a ripple effect on all that observe or participate in the original act.

In addition to creating a climate of trust, our own trust-ready behavior will attract others of similar behavior. Persons looking for trusting relationships will have an affinity toward our behavior. Watching our trustworthiness and wanting a like response, they seek a match. Already a bias for an open, honest, and direct relationship is generated. Others who are less trustworthy will see our high degree of commitment, consistency, and capability as a threat. We don't see trust readiness as being gullible. We believe, rather, that it helps us know what trusting behavior to expect from others. We know it because we demonstrate trust in our own behavior. We know a fraud more readily because we have worked to take the fraudulent, untrustworthy behavior out of our repertoire.

Another psychological principle can be leveraged to help us move toward trustworthiness. Human beings desire consistency between word and deed because it takes the guesswork out of situations. We apply this to ourselves as well as others. When we write down the commitments to ourselves to improve certain aspects of our trustworthiness, or for that matter, our trust willingness, we work to meet those commitments both consciously and subconsciously. And if our inner voice is alive and working, we will hold ourselves to the commitments. This is why writing down agreements for self-improvement is so important. We paint a new self-image of a more trustworthy person, and then we strive to meet our own, newly defined image. Having a fleeting thought about improvement doesn't have the same intensity as writing down commitments and reviewing progress.

Wise managers use this appreciation for consistency with their employees. Helping employees paint strong, positive self-images enables workers to perform wisely and competently in the absence of supervision. Good managers point to poor behavior as inconsistent with desirable behavior. "Jack, it's not like you to miss deadlines. You are always so organized." However, when we let our frustrations get the better of us and chastise by associating the employee with the undesirable behavior, it reinforces what we don't want. "Jack, I might have known you wouldn't have this done on time." Helping to paint a negative self-image in Jack will encourage him subtly to maintain consistency of image and deed. He will work to be disorganized or unreliable without realizing it consciously.

Painting a positive self-image for ourselves concerning trust readiness will find us working to live up to that image, without realizing it consciously. We will match image with deed. Remove the self-deprecating thinking and reflection. Replace it with a commitment to improve and fulfill the promise of trustworthiness and trust willingness.

The Self assessment in Appendix A provides a first step in developing your trust readiness by exposing your strengths and weaknesses. When you are ready to take action to improve your trust-inhibiting behaviors, practice the thoughts, "It is like me to be honest, to be trustworthy, to command the trust of others, and to deliver on the commitments I make." You may be surprised how fast you will pull yourself in line with this self-image.

## Determine Direction

Critical to improving upon trust is to know the context in which it is being sought. Knowing where you are going in life gives a framework for the role of trust in your life. To develop knowledge concerning your direction in life, you may find the Conceptual Image Document (CID) included in Appendix B of use. The CID provides structure to the discovery/clarification process. The CID poses a series of questions, arranged in four parts, which allow for long-term reflection and a review of supportive short-term goals/actions.

The thrust of the reflection is to bring to consciousness a purpose for being and to facilitate consistency of near-term actions. The understanding of our life's purpose provides perspective for our daily living. Our unique insight into our individual life's purpose provides strength and direction.

Such a process is important because when we are clear about our purpose in life, others increase their trust in us. People know where we are coming from with our words and actions. They begin to see the uniformity between our direction in life and our actions. We are more dependable and reliable when we make commitments because the commitments are in order with our reason for being. An internal integrity forms. In both subtle and bold ways this internal integrity is conveyed to those around us.

This moves us into a state of being. Living in a state of being means living in accordance with our life's purpose, living with integrity. Living with integrity provides strength and confidence that can eliminate concerns about the past or the future. People get the message that we know where we are going and are acting accordingly. The having and doing of daily life does not confuse others about who we are. Our possessions, academic degrees, positional honors constitute our havings. Our actions in our careers and our avocations constitute our doings. But because we are so clear on our individual reasons for being, our being comes across much stronger than what we have or what we do. We are in a state of being. We are human beings, not a human doings or a human havings. The state of being gives the people around us trust in our knowledge of self and confidence that we will live in conformance with that purpose.

Now when we add passion to this state of being, we find ourselves transmitting a clear and powerful message. We convey energy for life. We demonstrate a passion for being, being in the present, being in connection with the person present in front of us. Displaying that passion for life, focusing it on another and getting an understanding of who they are leads to rapid relationship building. Since we are exposed, open for all to see what we are about, others are drawn to the clarity and strength of willingness to show vulnerability. Fertile ground for trust has been created. Growing trust is not guaranteed in this instance, but the prospects are great given the condition of the soil.

Determining our direction holds one additional benefit. In Alden Hayashi's article, "When to Trust Your Gut," the proposition is put forth that our emotions and feelings may be essential to our intuitive ability to make good decisions.[2] We clearly understand that our left brain's logical and rational thinking is used in competent decision making. However, our right brain also holds much power. The ability to see complex patterns and broaden sensory perception describes some of this power. And since our brains are connected through an extensive nervous system to other parts of our bodies, including our guts, we truly get bodily signals or "gut" reactions. These gut reactions serve as a competitive edge in business, according to Hayashi's research.

The problem is, trusting our "gut" is susceptible to one major flaw. Using our emotions and feelings in decision making is useful when we know their origin, but being unconscious about what drives us, not having a direction but simply being reactive, puts us on a collision course with ill-advised decisions born out of indeterminate emotions. In other words, to use the power of our right brain, to read the signals or to trust our guts, we must understand ourselves. Thus, the drive to determine direction is essential to knowing self and being able to effectively tap into our intuition, and not having our undiscovered emotions drive our actions. So, in trusting our gut to trust someone else, knowing ourselves is crucial.

# DEVELOPING INTERPERSONAL RELATIONSHIPS

The two strategies for developing trust in your relationships with others are fairly intuitive but bear explanation. The first strategy is to have the intention to create trust and the second calls for continually investing in it.

## Have an Intention to Create Trust

While clarity about our own trust readiness is an important first step, it will not assure that trust will always be extended or earned. The only guarantee to trusting relationships is our perseverance and tenacity in the face of obstacles. Rarely do our trust-building efforts go as planned. We are forming relationships with willful persons, others that also have the creative willpower to produce or avoid trust; to make decisions to trust or not; to act in trustworthy or untrustworthy ways. Even with the best of aims, they are as likely as we are to make mistakes along the way.

Achieving trust is decidedly a function of our willingness to overcome the barriers presented. The impediments and obstacles simply denote the price we will have to pay in terms of willpower and focus to achieve trust. Are we saying we can form trust with anyone, regardless of differences and obstructions? In a word, yes. Nelson Mandela formed trust with his guards on Robins Island. It took perseverance, dedication, and interpersonal mastery, but creating trust in such a harsh environment prepared him to build trust with an entire nation as well as with his former nemesis. Forming trust with P. W. Botha and later with F. W. DeKlerk to lead South Africa out of fear and division took focus, resolve, and a clear and honest vision of who he was and what he wanted. Martin Luther King Jr. provided another model for building trust in the face of adversity. He understood all too well the hard work involved in bridging the huge divide between blacks and whites and called upon people to join him in this labor:

> *God, who gave us minds for thinking and bodies for working, would defeat his own purpose if he permitted us to obtain through prayer what may come through work and intelligence. Prayer is a marvelous and necessary supplement of our feeble efforts, but it is a dangerous substitute. . . . I am certain we need to pray for God's help and guidance in this integration struggle, but we are gravely misled if we think the struggle will be won only by prayer.*[3]

While it is far easier and momentarily more gratifying to just give the establishment a piece of our minds, it will not move us closer to the result we claim to want.

In order to establish trust in difficult situations, we must understand our competing desires. Building trust is not compatible with vengeful desires, however justified they may seem. Neither is building trust compatible with our desires to manipulate or play up our own ego. Frequently we say we want trust, but are unwilling to follow through when barriers appear. It is not that we are immoral or terrible people. We simply underestimate the barriers or overestimate our willingness. We can learn from our failed attempts to build trust, but only when we see our connection to the failure. Blaming others may give us a short reprieve from some type of strange guilt, but it will not give us the insight to produce better results the next time. We are not mandated to produce trust with everyone, but if we are willing, we can.

We have seen people mindlessly hope for trust to materialize in dysfunctional relationships. Leaders, who loathe admitting that trust is low in their organization despite hard evidence to the contrary, will lapse into wishful thinking, hoping good fortune will magically reverse the situation. But by failing to take responsible action, they not only waste valuable time but also contribute to the cynicism that created mistrust in the first place. Facing up to the work that is necessary to build trust in organizations is admittedly daunting, especially because of the personal commitment required of leaders.

Understanding our connection to all that we create, including broken relationships, is characteristic of intentional living. We know that either consciously or unconsciously, we have produced all the relationships we experience. They are of our making. True, other parties exert their own intentions in a relationship, but we have no control over that. What we do control is the effort and energy we bring or withhold. Two tools that will be of use in determining your intention to create trust are the "Key Relationships and Trust" and "Enhancing Team Trust," both of which are found in Appendix B.

## Invest Continually

Having achieved a high level of trust in a relationship, enjoying the emotional fruits of the investment, we may find ourselves believing the work is done. Far from it. Continual investment is required. Time and change cause common goals and commitments to evolve and capabilities to grow or diminish. And while people may behave with consistency in stable environments, change and chaos disrupt our predictability. Without continued investment, entropy works to deconstruct the trust that was of such value.

As the philosopher Alan Watts said, you don't sing a song to get to the end of it. We form trusting relationships to enjoy the fruits of the bonding. And wanting the relationship to continue, we must realize the ongoing investment needed. Staying current with another human being necessitates time and energy. Continual investment is mandatory to maintain trust when goals shift, turns of life add complications, or daily struggles distract us from our relationships.

How do you stop the erosion of hard-won trust? The same strategies that build trust also maintain it. Honestly sharing your life's direction with another as it matures over time reconstitutes commitment to one another. Demonstrating support and loyalty to the emerging person in front of you sends the message of commitment. Spending time together and being aware of each other's development allows for knowledge, which enhances predictability and consistency. Learning what interests and developing skills are emerging from each other produces awareness of capabilities.

Consider how relationships between children and their parents mature in trust over time. Parents create a bond of trust through their love and caring of a child. And the parents' love and familiarity with the child reciprocally build trust. Maintaining that trust, as the child becomes a teen and the teen an adult, requires continual and mutual effort. We do not trust teens in the same way we trust our young children. Their capabilities are vastly different; their commitments evolve with new interests and new relationships; they have had many more years than the younger child to demonstrate more or less consistency in a variety of situations.

Certainly the learning from parents who have trusting and close relationships with their teenagers and adult children is the continued investments of time and interest are key in developing trust and close relationships. Knowing each other is not a one-shot occurrence; it is an ongoing endeavor. Part of this continual investment requires challenging our own assumptions and beliefs to see what barriers we create to trust. Use the "Ladder of Inference," "Uncovering Assumptions That Block Trust," and "Dialogue That Builds Trust" tools in Appendix B to help you reveal your own barriers.

# DEVELOPING THE INSTITUTION

Knowing the considerable work required in establishing high levels of trust with others and self gives us a sense of the complexity of growing trust in an organization. How do we move the institution toward a culture of trust? We suggest two broad strategies: seeing anew and reformulating for trust.

## Seeing Anew

Within an organization, we may become blind to the many messages that scream distrust to the workforce. Distrust can be so entrenched in our policies and structures, our management philosophies and organizational norms, that we become inured to it. If we stop and watch for these messages, we can begin to see the organization anew, and begin to detect the overtones of mistrust that are present in everyday work (Figure 6.2).

Consider some of these common practices:

- Multiple signatures on purchase requests

- Monitored communications

- Redundant roles and duplicated functions

- Quality control and inspections

- Limited access to information

- Communication channels that flow down through a hierarchy

**Figure 6.2**   Examining your organization.

While many of these practices may be prudent and sometimes even necessary, you need to be mindful of the message of distrust that goes with them.

What sends a message of trust in an organization? Trust can be built in a myriad of ways both small and large. One company we encountered in our research kept a container of umbrellas in the foyer of their office building inviting people to use and return them as needed. A more significant practice drives decision-making authority down to the shop floor level, indicating trust in the ability and wisdom of the frontline employee. Some organizations open their books for employees to see or invite employees to participate in shaping the vision and direction of the organization. This sends the message that employees are trusted as valued business partners.

Take, for example, the time-honored and nearly universal policy of keeping salaries secret from employees in an organization. While these policies do protect individual privacy and minimize an organization's exposure to headhunters, it sends an unmistakable message that the organization does not trust employees to handle such information maturely or appropriately. At least one organization sees it differently. Dennis Bakke, CEO of AES Corporation—a $6.7 billion global electricity company with 53,000 employees, believes everyone's pay should be published. Bakke admits that such openness may be more difficult for managers, but, he believes, it leads to a healthier work environment. His experience has been that creating a trusting, engaging, and rewarding place to work has made pay issues less consequential and performance higher.[4]

Seeing anew is about looking at the organization's daily operation through the eyes of trust. What trust messages are being sent? What messages of distrust are conveyed? This is not to say that the current procedures, policies, protocols, and structures don't serve a purpose. They may well have been put into place for excellent reasons. We are asking for a focus on their impact in producing a trust-biased organization, an organization that sends and reinforces a trust expectation. The first step is to see the environment anew. We only create confusion when we display inconsistent behavior in calling for trust but building a chorus of distrustful messages. Our tool, "Examining Organizational Practices" will help you sort out those practices that contribute to trust and those that inhibit it.

## Reformulating for Trust

Once we see anew the inconsistency between our claim of trust and the messages coming forth from the institution, we can begin to plan for improvement. We must reformulate the organization to include the trust ingredient in abundance. The organization needs to reek of trust! This move to trust must be taken, however, with the understanding of why the distrust signals were created in the first place. There must have been some benefit in the policies, procedures, structure, and culture that were put into place. We want to reformulate the organization for trust without losing these benefits.

The transformation called for by this strategy of reformulating for trust will be specific to the situation of an organization. Appendix B explains in some detail the approach we most commonly take with clients to shepherd this process. See the tool titled "Reformulating for Trust" in Appendix B.

## TOOLS FOR DEVELOPING TRUST

We have just addressed key strategies for developing trust: look inside, risk for trust, determine direction, create trust and invest continually, see anew, and reformulate for trust. These strategies can be supported with a myriad of *trust tools*, tools that help to create trust. In Appendix B we have included a collection of trust-building tools many of which have been referenced in the chapter. This collection is neither an exclusive nor exhaustive set, but rather a starting place for building a personal set of exercises and creative methods. We have tried to provide a variety of tools in the hopes that at least one will suit each reader's situation. The introduction to Appendix B will help you determine which tool will be most appropriate to your trust-building need.

While any of the tools will begin to move you toward trust, we urge you to consider the framework and strategies for developing trust prior to simply picking up an attractive tool. We have seen tools used to temporarily excite a team or group of workshop attendees, but with little long-term impact offered because they were not connected to an underlying strategy. Begin with the proper diagnostic work to discover where trust problems exist, formulate a strategy to address them, and then select a tool that best meets your need.

## CONCLUSIONS

Trust is a journey of relationship building, with self and others. Knowing how to perform trust assessments and understanding the elements of trust are useful when followed by real action. Building our own trust readiness is an important first step, but will only result in real change when followed with deliberate action. Maintaining trust once achieved requires a continual investment. The investment in trust is further challenged by changes in environment; circumstances; or peoples' needs, capabilities, and intentions.

# KEY POINTS

- Look inside to build trustworthiness with self and with respect to others

- Work to determine your direction or life's purpose, and create a clear path to creating trust with others

- Ongoing relationships call upon us to invest continually with our time and energies to produce trust

- Ultimately, the level of trust we have in any relationship is a product of our intentions

- In organizations, identify those practices that erode trust and replace them or mitigate them with policies and practices that reinforce trust

- Reformulate the organization's structure, culture, and leadership approach to create a trustful work environment

# ENDNOTES

1. R. B. Cialdini, *Influence: Science and Practice* (New York: HarperCollins, 1993).
2. A. M. Hayashi, "When to Trust Your Gut," *Harvard Business Review* 79, no. 2 (2001).
3. L. Hoskins, ed. *"I Have a Dream," The quotations of Martin Luther King Jr.* (New York: Grosset & Dunlap, 1968).
4. D. Bakke, "HBR Case Study," *Harvard Business Review* (May 2001): 46.

# Epilogue

We have covered much concerning the subject of trust. But one important area we haven't addressed is the area of trust with something larger than a group of people or an organization. It involves developing trust with a deity, a destiny, or the universe. Its omission is not a reflection of its importance, but rather a recognition that this facet of trust deserves much more than this text has to offer. This profound aspect of trust manifests in our lives as faith, and represents a level of trust that requires a tremendous amount of conviction.

Perhaps the most famous example of this level of faith and trust is Mother Teresa. Born in 1910 as Agnes Bojaxhiu in Skopje, Macedonia, she was sent to Calcutta in 1929 under the care and guidance of the church. In 1930 she took her permanent vows and the name Teresa. At first she worked in a Catholic school for girls in Calcutta, serving in the Loreto convent. She had a reasonably protected life in the convent as she assisted students from well-to-do families of European descent. The convent was surrounded by a large wall keeping the outside world at a safe distance.

She tells of the signal from God she received during a train ride. It was a call to action, asking her to put her full trust in her God. She stated that it was the hardest single action of her life—to obey and trust God on this matter—much harder than her vows. On August 16, 1948, she went outside the protection of the walled convent to aid the poorest of the poor, the sickest of the sick, the outcasts of an impoverished society. She was called to serve in a different capacity, forming The Missionaries of Charity. She led the Missionary Sisters and later the Missionary Brothers of Charity in administering to the dying, the hungry, the poor. The Nobel Peace Prize awarded her in 1979 demonstrated that the world had a firm grasp on her commitment, her capability, her consistency in her life's mission. But it must not be over-looked that the mission was made possible by an act of faith, a trust in something bigger than our seen reality.[1]

The connection with a more powerful source is found in nearly all cultures and spiritual beliefs. In the Buddhist tradition, The Dalai Lama speaks of the awakening mind as the intention to achieve Buddha-hood, saying, "The awakening mind is like an elixir that can transform base iron into gold. This is because when we cultivate the awakening mind within ourselves, even our external behavior, the way we speak and the way we behave toward other people can be transformed."[2]

In other words, seeking a trusting relationship with a power beyond ourselves has a transforming impact on our lives and on our relationships. Trusting in something greater and unseen holds the promise for many of building trust with the human relations that can be seen. Trusting a higher power is a choice. Looking to form relationships with something greater will call upon a level of trust unmatched in the simple human experience.

# ENDNOTES

1. J. L. Gonzalez-Balado, *Mother Teresa: In My Own Words* (Hodder & Stoughton, 1996).
2. His Holiness, The Dalai Lama of Tibet, *The Joy of Living and Dying in Peace* (San Francisco: Harper Collins, 1997): 21.

# Additional Resources

Cialdini, R. B. *Influence: Science and Practice.* New York: HarperCollins, 1993.

Coutu, D. L. "Trust in Virtual Teams." *Harvard Business Review* 76, no. 3 (1998).

De Furia, G. L. *Facilitator's Guide to the Interpersonal Trust Surveys.* San Francisco: Jossey-Bass/Pfeiffer, 1996.

Gonzalez-Balado, J. L. *Mother Teresa: In My Own Words.* Hodder & Stoughton, 1996.

Kohen D. "Trust and Business: Barriers and Bridges." *Business & Professional Ethics Journal* 16, no. 1–3 (1997).

Reina, D. and M. Reina. *Trust & Betrayal in the Workplace.* San Francisco: Berrett-Koehler, 1990.

Sheppard, B. H. and D. M. Sherman. "The Grammar of Trust: A Model and General Implications." *The Academy of Management Review* 23, no. 3 (1998).

# Appendix A

# Trust Assessments

## IMPLEMENTING THE
## TRUST ASSESSMENTS

The assessments that follow are designed to help you diagnose not only the level of trust in your targeted relationship, but also the attributes or trust components most in need of attention. We recommend that every reader of this book take the Self assessment as an exercise in personal development. Beyond that, identify the level or relationship in which trust is a concern for you and select the assessment that matches that level or addresses your area of concern. Use the table below to help you identify the appropriate assessment.

| If your concern is with . . . | Then use the . . . |
|---|---|
| One other person | Person to Person assessment |
| A team of people | Within Teams assessment |
| Another team or department | Team to Team assessment |
| The whole organization | Organization assessment |
| Another organization | Organization to Organization assessment |

The assessment process is an important first step in building trust. Done carelessly, however, it can do more harm than good. If you involve others in this assessment process, do so in a manner that protects and honors those you will ask to participate. Delving into people's perceptions about the trust-worthiness of others has the potential for opening up volatile issues and strong emotions. We include here a set of instructions and considerations for responsible application of these assessments.

# INSTRUCTIONS FOR USE

## Determine Who Should Participate

Participation in the assessment process depends on which perspective of trust you are addressing. Obviously if the concern is between individuals, those two people should be encouraged to take the Person to Person assessment with their particular relationship in mind. Where team trust is involved, it will be necessary to use the Within Teams assessment with the whole team. As the population increases to span departments or the whole organization, you may be forced to survey a representative sampling of the population. If your population size is small (less than 30 people), it should be possible for everyone to take the assessment. On the other hand, if you are assessing an entire organization of thousands, you may only need to take a random sample. As the number of respondents increases, so does your work compiling the results.

If you decide to take a sampling, it is important to select a large enough number of people so that the results accurately represent the population. Once you have determined your sample size, decide on a way of randomly selecting the respondents. You want to select a method that will not bias your results. For instance, sampling the first 30 people who come into the manager's office is not a good method because it would tend to bias the results toward those who have a good relationship with the manager or whose job responsibilities involve frequent contact with the manager.

Random sampling methods may include:

- Picking every third employee number

- Listing employees in alphabetical order and picking every fourth name

- Selecting all employees on each shift who have a social security number ending in an odd number

Make sure that you sample a good cross section of employees, picking people at all levels, positions, shifts, and so on.

## Segment the Data

Segmenting of data is necessary only when using the Organization assesment. When assessing a whole organization, you must decide to what level of detail you want to segment the data. In other words, in addition to looking at the results of the organization as a whole, you may want to examine results for individual portions of the organization. Segmenting options include (but are not limited to):

- By level in the organization (managers versus employees)

- By department or function

- By bargaining unit

- By job classification (for example, secretaries, operators, engineers)

- By shift

Of course, these are not mutually exclusive; you can combine segmentation methods as you see fit.

You want to segment the data into enough groups so that you can pinpoint areas of strength and weakness. For instance, it may be useful to know that only Department A perceives the organization as having low trust while Department B rated the organization favorably. However, you don't want to segment the data so much that you compromise the confidentiality and anonymity of the responses. For instance, if one segment is Engineering but you only have one or two engineers, the responses could no longer be considered anonymous. Since the information in the assessment can be sensitive, maintaining anonymity can lead to more honest responses.

Once you have decided how you want to segment the data, you must figure out how to mark the forms so that you will know to which segment each form belongs. You want to do this in such a way that it does not raise fear or suspicion in the respondents that their responses will not be confidential. This can be achieved by color-coding the forms or providing coded envelopes.

## Distribute the Assessments

Next you must decide how to have the assessments distributed. Options include:

- Having someone not in the chain of command pass the forms out in a meeting

- Sending out the forms with return envelopes

- Having a manager or supervisor hand out the forms

In general, the first method is the best. If one person conducts the meetings that introduce the assessment and explain the process, then all respondents will get the same information. Someone outside the chain of command may be less intimidating than the respondents' supervisor. The meeting format enables you to explain the purpose of the assessment and answer questions about the forms. It also ensures that the forms will be completed and returned. If you cannot conduct the assessment in this manner, make sure that thorough instructions accompany the assessment.

## Introduce the Assessment

When you distribute the assessment, you should provide the respondents this information:

- Why you are conducting the assessment
- How you intend to use the information
- How their anonymity and confidentiality will be maintained
- The importance of their providing honest, open responses
- When they can expect to receive the results

You should also explain the instructions thoroughly and explain who they should be thinking of when they complete the form—who "we" is and who "our leaders" are. Usually "we" represents their immediate work group but this definition may vary depending on your purpose or segmentation. Before respondents begin, ask them to review all the items. Explain any items that people find confusing.

# ETHICAL CONSIDERATIONS

It is important to consider your obligation to the people whose input you solicit. It is our opinion that any time you ask employees for their input you are obliged to report back to them on the results and responses in a timely fashion. Ideally, you should report first to those who have taken the time to participate in the process. If you are required to share results first with the leadership of your organization, you should make sure that they accept the obligation to share the analysis with the respondents and commit to act on the results.

When conducting an organizationwide assessment, the results should be reported back to everyone in the organization. As mentioned earlier, the best option is to report first to those who participated in the assessment.

You may want to do this by pulling everyone together and presenting the information to all at one time. However you decide to report this information, you should get back to people in a timely manner and provide a two-way exchange.

# PLANNING FOR FOLLOW-UP

How you handle follow-up will vary widely depending on your population size and other factors. However, you should include the following actions as part of a comprehensive follow-up report:

- Review the assessment process—explain how you gathered the data and why

- Review the components of trust and the model that underlies the assessments

- Present the results and explain how to read any charts or graphs

- Give people time to assimilate the data and express their interpretation

- Decide or present a future course of action

As you present the results, you should be prepared to handle some tough situations. Helping people understand the use and value of the assessment is a good foundation for heading off any sticky situations. The data should not be used to "rate" trust, but to help people identify where they should focus their learning and development. No matter how positive an organization's culture is, there is always need for improvement. This assessment process is designed to help your organization identify those areas and make best use of your improvement efforts.

# TRUST ASSESSMENT

## SELF

This questionnaire is designed to assess your own level of trust performance. Answering honestly is the first step to building your capacity for trust. There are two parts to this assessment. The first part asks you to take a quick overall measure of your trust performance—that is both your trustworthiness and your willingness to enter into trusting relationships. The second part dissects trust into its six component parts and helps you assess your level of ability in each part by asking you to identify where on a continuum of behavior you feel you fall.

If you would like to take this assessment to the next level, consider asking someone else to complete the assessment for you. This will give you feedback about how others perceive you and how close your own perception of self aligns with your appearance to others.

### PART ONE: OVERALL ASSESSMENT

On a scale of 1–7 how do you rate your own trust performance?

| Completely Mistrustful and Untrustworthy | 1 | 2 | 3 | 4 | 5 | 6 | 7 | Highly Trusting and Trustworthy |

On a scale of 1–7 what level of trust performance would you like to demonstrate?

| Completely Mistrustful and Untrustworthy | 1 | 2 | 3 | 4 | 5 | 6 | 7 | Highly Trusting and Trustworthy |

### PART TWO: TRUST COMPONENT ASSESSMENT

The following questions will help you identify the domains in which your trust performance is strongest and weakest. The contrasting descriptions are designed to provoke your thinking regarding trust. For each row, indicate the point on the continuum (from 1 to 7) that best describes you. A "1" indicates that the description on the left describes you perfectly. A "7" means that you match the description on the right. If neither provides a perfect description, use the rest of the scale to indicate where between the two extremes you think you fall. Circle your answers and calculate your totals for each element of trust.

# Trustworthiness

## Capability

| | | | | | | | | |
|---|---|---|---|---|---|---|---|---|
| 1. I keep my shortcomings hidden from others. | 1 | 2 | 3 | 4 | 5 | 6 | 7 | I am honest with everyone about what I can and cannot do. |
| 2. I lack the skills I need to fulfill my obligations. | 1 | 2 | 3 | 4 | 5 | 6 | 7 | I have both the technical and inter-personal skills to fulfill my obligations. |
| 3. I am a poor listener. | 1 | 2 | 3 | 4 | 5 | 6 | 7 | I listen empathically to others. |
| 4. I do just enough to get by. | 1 | 2 | 3 | 4 | 5 | 6 | 7 | I do my best in all situations. |
| 5. I don't often offer helpful feedback to others. | 1 | 2 | 3 | 4 | 5 | 6 | 7 | I frequently give others pointed and helpful feedback. |

**Total Score:**

## Commitment

| | | | | | | | | |
|---|---|---|---|---|---|---|---|---|
| 6. I talk about others behind their backs. | 1 | 2 | 3 | 4 | 5 | 6 | 7 | I am loyal to people even when we are not together. |
| 7. I often belittle the views of others. | 1 | 2 | 3 | 4 | 5 | 6 | 7 | I demonstrate respect for others' views, beliefs, and ideas. |
| 8. I withhold my points of view from others. | 1 | 2 | 3 | 4 | 5 | 6 | 7 | I openly share my ideas even when they are different. |
| 9. I act without consideration for others. | 1 | 2 | 3 | 4 | 5 | 6 | 7 | Before I act, I take the feelings and welfare of others into consideration. |
| 10. I ignore poor performance and broken promises. | 1 | 2 | 3 | 4 | 5 | 6 | 7 | I hold people accountable for living up to our agreements. |
| 11. I consider only my own development needs. | 1 | 2 | 3 | 4 | 5 | 6 | 7 | I support the professional and personal development of others. |

**Total Score:**

## Consistency

| | | | | | | | | |
|---|---|---|---|---|---|---|---|---|
| 12. No one can tell where I stand. | 1 | 2 | 3 | 4 | 5 | 6 | 7 | I say what I mean and mean what I say. |
| 13. I do not reliably keep my commitments. | 1 | 2 | 3 | 4 | 5 | 6 | 7 | I follow through on my commitments 100 percent. |
| 14. My output is uneven and unpredictable. | 1 | 2 | 3 | 4 | 5 | 6 | 7 | I deliver the same level of effort in my work 100 percent of the time. |

*Continued*

| 15. What I do doesn't match what I say. | 1 2 3 4 5 6 7 | I walk my talk. |
|---|---|---|
| 16. My positions vary from day to day. | 1 2 3 4 5 6 7 | My positions are consistent with my espoused core values. |

Total Score: _____

## Trust Willingness

### Willingness to Invest

| 17. I am thoughtless about forming trust with others. | 1 2 3 4 5 6 7 | I have an accurate assessment of the level of trust I intend to build. |
|---|---|---|
| 18. I believe trust will just happen over time. | 1 2 3 4 5 6 7 | I have an accurate assessment of what it will take to build trust. |
| 19. I am passive in my approach to building trust. | 1 2 3 4 5 6 7 | I take active steps to build trust with others. |

Total Score: _____

### Willingness to Examine Assumptions

| 20. I am unwilling to question my beliefs. | 1 2 3 4 5 6 7 | I continually challenge my own assumptions. |
|---|---|---|
| 21. I stick to my strongly held positions. | 1 2 3 4 5 6 7 | I am open to changing my points of view. |
| 22. I am suspicious of the motives of others. | 1 2 3 4 5 6 7 | I give people the benefit of the doubt. |
| 23. I avoid getting honest feedback. | 1 2 3 4 5 6 7 | I seek input and feedback from others. |
| 24. I hide or cover up my mistakes. | 1 2 3 4 5 6 7 | I freely admit when I am wrong. |
| 25. My relationships are based on my assumptions and biases about people. | 1 2 3 4 5 6 7 | I harbor no prejudices about others that negatively impact my relationships. |

Total Score: _____

### Willingness to Risk

| 26. I tend to be blind to opportunities that present themselves. | 1 2 3 4 5 6 7 | I continually look for opportunities to change or improve. |
|---|---|---|
| 27. I always take the safest path. | 1 2 3 4 5 6 7 | I am willing to risk failure to try new things. |

| | | | | | | | | |
|---|---|---|---|---|---|---|---|---|
| 28. There are certain things I won't talk about with anyone. | 1 | 2 | 3 | 4 | 5 | 6 | 7 | I can talk about anything. |
| 29. I tend to hoard or withhold information. | 1 | 2 | 3 | 4 | 5 | 6 | 7 | I freely share all information; nothing is secret with me. |
| 30. I trust no decision made without my own input and influence. | 1 | 2 | 3 | 4 | 5 | 6 | 7 | I frequently trust others to make decisions on my behalf. |
| 31. Two strikes and you're through. | 1 | 2 | 3 | 4 | 5 | 6 | 7 | I grant others mistakes without it affecting my level of trust. |
| 32. Trust goes to zero in new situations. | 1 | 2 | 3 | 4 | 5 | 6 | 7 | I readily trust even in new situations. |

**Total Score:**

# PART THREE: ASSESSING THE RESULTS

Enter your total score for each section in the score column and divide by the number of items in that section to obtain an average for each component that matches our 1–7 scale. Then total the three scores in each section and divide by the total number of items for that portion of the assessment to get a score for both trustworthiness and willingness to trust.

| | Score | # of Items | Result |
|---|---|---|---|
| Capability | | ÷ 5 | |
| Commitment | | ÷ 6 | |
| Consistency | | ÷ 5 | |
| **Trustworthiness** | | ÷ 16 | |
| Willingness to invest | | ÷ 3 | |
| Willingness to examine assumptions | | ÷ 6 | |
| Willingness to risk | | ÷ 7 | |
| **Trust Willingness** | | ÷ 16 | |

*Continued*

Compare your calculated component score with your initial overall assessment in Part One. Does your calculated component score match your initial estimate of the current level of trust? How large is the gap between the calculated score and the level of trust you want to have? Use the component scores and the suggested tools to design a strategy for building trust.

## Tool Suggestions

Consider using the following tools to help you build your trust capacity:

- Life Plan
- Ladder of Inference
- Left Hand Column

# TRUST ASSESSMENT

## PERSON TO PERSON

This questionnaire is designed to help you build trust in a relationship with one particular person. There are two parts to this assessment. The first part asks you to take a quick overall measure of your level of trust with your chosen person. The second part dissects trust into its six component parts and helps you assess where your relationship is strongest and weakest.

### PART ONE: OVERALL ASSESSMENT

On a scale of 1–7, how do you rate your current level of trust with this person?

| Strong Mistrust | 1 | 2 | 3 | Neutral 4 | 5 | 6 | 7 | High Trust |
|---|---|---|---|---|---|---|---|---|

On a scale of 1–7, what level would you like your trust with this person to be?

| Strong Mistrust | 1 | 2 | 3 | Neutral 4 | 5 | 6 | 7 | High Trust |
|---|---|---|---|---|---|---|---|---|

### PART TWO: TRUST COMPONENT ASSESSMENT

The following questions will help you identify the domains in which your trust is strongest and weakest. The contrasting descriptions are designed to provoke your thinking regarding trust. For each row, indicate the point on the continuum (from 1 to 7) that best describes this relationship. A "1" indicates that the description on the left describes the relationship perfectly. A "7" means that you match the description on the right. If neither provides a perfect description, use the rest of the scale to indicate where between the two extremes you think you fall. Circle your answers and calculate your totals for each element of trust.

#### Trustworthiness

**Capability**

| 1. We hide our shortcomings from each other. | 1 2 3 4 5 6 7 | We are honest with each other about what each of us can and cannot do. |
|---|---|---|

*Continued*

| | 1 | 2 | 3 | 4 | 5 | 6 | 7 | |
|---|---|---|---|---|---|---|---|---|
| 2. We lack the skills it will take to fulfill our obligations to each other. | 1 | 2 | 3 | 4 | 5 | 6 | 7 | We both have the technical skills we need to fulfill our obligations. |
| 3. We have no solid knowledge of each other's competence. | 1 | 2 | 3 | 4 | 5 | 6 | 7 | We have clearly demonstrated our competence to each other. |
| 4. We seldom hear what the other is saying. | 1 | 2 | 3 | 4 | 5 | 6 | 7 | We listen empathically to each other. |
| 5. We do just enough to get by. | 1 | 2 | 3 | 4 | 5 | 6 | 7 | We both work to be our best. |
| 6. We seldom provide each other feedback and when we do it is confusing or hurtful. | 1 | 2 | 3 | 4 | 5 | 6 | 7 | We frequently give each other pointed and helpful feedback. |

**Total Score:**

## Commitment

| | 1 | 2 | 3 | 4 | 5 | 6 | 7 | |
|---|---|---|---|---|---|---|---|---|
| 7. We talk about each other behind our backs. | 1 | 2 | 3 | 4 | 5 | 6 | 7 | We are loyal to each other even when we are not together. |
| 8. We often belittle each others' views. | 1 | 2 | 3 | 4 | 5 | 6 | 7 | We demonstrate respect for each others' views, beliefs, and ideas. |
| 9. We withhold our points of view from each other. | 1 | 2 | 3 | 4 | 5 | 6 | 7 | We openly share our ideas even when they are different from each other. |
| 10. We act without consideration for each other. | 1 | 2 | 3 | 4 | 5 | 6 | 7 | Before we act, we take the feelings and welfare of the other person into consideration. |
| 11. Our individual commitments lie outside of this relationship. | 1 | 2 | 3 | 4 | 5 | 6 | 7 | We are committed to achieving our common goals. |
| 12. We ignore poor performance and broken promises. | 1 | 2 | 3 | 4 | 5 | 6 | 7 | We hold one another accountable for living up to our agreements. |
| 13. We undermine the development efforts of the other person. | 1 | 2 | 3 | 4 | 5 | 6 | 7 | We support each other's professional and personal development. |

**Total Score:**

## Consistency

| | 1 | 2 | 3 | 4 | 5 | 6 | 7 | |
|---|---|---|---|---|---|---|---|---|
| 14. No one could tell where either of us stands. | 1 | 2 | 3 | 4 | 5 | 6 | 7 | We each say what we mean and mean what we say. |
| 15. Neither of us keeps our commitments. | 1 | 2 | 3 | 4 | 5 | 6 | 7 | Each of us follows through on our commitments 100 percent. |

| 16. Our output is uneven and unpredictable. | 1 2 3 4 5 6 7 | We both deliver the same level of effort in our work 100 percent of the time. |
|---|---|---|
| 17. What we each do doesn't match what we say. | 1 2 3 4 5 6 7 | We each walk our talk. |
| 18. Our positions vary depending on the person we are talking to. | 1 2 3 4 5 6 7 | Our positions are consistent with our espoused core values. |

**Total Score:**

## Trust Willingness

### Willingness to Invest

| 19. We are thoughtless about forming trust with the other person. | 1 2 3 4 5 6 7 | We each have an accurate assessment of the level of trust we intend to build and understand why we need to build it. |
|---|---|---|
| 20. We believe trust will just happen over time. | 1 2 3 4 5 6 7 | We each have an accurate assessment of what it will take to build trust. |
| 21. We are passive in our approach to building trust. | 1 2 3 4 5 6 7 | We each take active steps to build trust with each other. |

**Total Score:**

### Willingness to Examine Assumptions

| 22. Neither of us is willing to question our beliefs. | 1 2 3 4 5 6 7 | We continually challenge our own assumptions. |
|---|---|---|
| 23. We each stick to our strongly held positions. | 1 2 3 4 5 6 7 | We are open to changing our points of view. |
| 24. We are suspicious of the other's motives. | 1 2 3 4 5 6 7 | We give each other the benefit of the doubt. |
| 25. We avoid getting honest feedback. | 1 2 3 4 5 6 7 | We seek input and feedback from each other |
| 26. We hide or cover up our mistakes from each other. | 1 2 3 4 5 6 7 | We freely admit when we are wrong. |
| 27. Our relationship is based on our assumptions and biases. | 1 2 3 4 5 6 7 | We harbor no prejudices about each other that negatively impact our relationship. |

**Total Score:**

### Willingness to Risk

| 28. We are blind to opportunities that present themselves. | 1 2 3 4 5 6 7 | We continually look for opportunities to innovate or improve. |
|---|---|---|

*Continued*

| 29. We always take the safest path. | 1  2  3  4  5  6  7 | We are willing to risk failure to try new things. |
|---|---|---|
| 30. Certain subjects are off-limits; we have undiscussible issues. | 1  2  3  4  5  6  7 | We have an open, honest climate; we can talk about anything. |
| 31. We tend to hoard or withhold information. | 1  2  3  4  5  6  7 | We freely share all information with each other; nothing is secret. |
| 32. We trust no decision made without our own input and influence. | 1  2  3  4  5  6  7 | Each of us is trusted to make decisions for the other. |
| 33. Two strikes and we're through. | 1  2  3  4  5  6  7 | We grant each other mistakes without it affecting our level of trust in each other. |
| 34. Trust goes to zero in new situations. | 1  2  3  4  5  6  7 | We readily trust each other even in new situations. |

**Total Score:**

## PART THREE: ASSESSING THE RESULTS

Enter your total score for each section in the score column and divide by the number of items in that section to obtain an average for each component that matches our 1–7 scale. Then total the three scores in each section and divide by the total number of items for that portion of the assessment to get a score for both trustworthiness and willingness to trust.

|  | Score | # of Items | Result |
|---|---|---|---|
| Capability |  | ÷ 6 |  |
| Commitment |  | ÷ 7 |  |
| Consistency |  | ÷ 5 |  |
| **Trustworthiness** |  | ÷ 18 |  |
| Willingness to invest |  | ÷ 3 |  |
| Willingness to examine assumptions |  | ÷ 6 |  |
| Willingness to risk |  | ÷ 7 |  |
| **Trust Willingness** |  | ÷ 16 |  |

Compare your calculated component score with your initial overall assessment in Part One. Does your calculated component score match your initial estimate of the current level of trust? How large is the gap between the calculated score and the level of trust you want to have? Use the component scores and the suggested tools to design a strategy for building trust.

## Tool Suggestions

Consider using the following tools to help you build your trust capacity:

- Key Relationship and Trust
- Dialogue
- Ladder of Inference
- Left Hand Column
- Purpose Hierarchy
- Interface Conflict Solving Model

# TRUST ASSESSMENT

# WITHIN TEAMS

This questionnaire is designed to assess trust within your team. There are two parts to this assessment. The first part asks you to take a quick overall measure of the level of trust within your team. The second part dissects trust into its six component parts and helps you assess where team trust is strongest and weakest. Answer all the questions carefully with your whole team in mind. You can repeat this questionnaire for all the teams of which you are a member.

## PART ONE: OVERALL ASSESSMENT

On a scale of 1–7, how high is the *current level* of trust within this team?

| Strong |   |   |   | Neutral |   |   |   | High |
|--------|---|---|---|---------|---|---|---|------|
| Mistrust | 1 | 2 | 3 | 4 | 5 | 6 | 7 | Trust |

On a scale of 1–7, how high does the level of trust within this team *need to be* to assure the achievement of your common purpose?

| Strong |   |   |   | Neutral |   |   |   | High |
|--------|---|---|---|---------|---|---|---|------|
| Mistrust | 1 | 2 | 3 | 4 | 5 | 6 | 7 | Trust |

## PART TWO: TRUST COMPONENT ASSESSMENT

The following questions will help you identify the domains in which your team's level of trust is strongest and weakest. The contrasting descriptions are designed to provoke your thinking regarding trust. For each row, indicate the point on the continuum (from 1 to 7) that best describes this team. A "1" indicates that the description on the left describes the team perfectly. A "7" means that your team matches the description on the right. If neither provides a perfect description, use the rest of the scale to indicate where between the two extremes you think you fall. Circle your answers and calculate your totals for each element of trust.

### Trustworthiness

**Capability**

| 1. We hide our shortcomings from each other. | 1 2 3 4 5 6 7 | We are honest with each other about what each of us can and cannot do. |
|---|---|---|

| 2. We lack the skills it will take to fulfill our purpose. | 1 2 3 4 5 6 7 | We all have the technical skills we need to fulfill our purpose. |
|---|---|---|
| 3. We have no solid knowledge of each other's competence. | 1 2 3 4 5 6 7 | We have all clearly demonstrated our competence to each other. |
| 4. We seldom hear what others are saying. | 1 2 3 4 5 6 7 | We are all empathic listeners. |
| 5. We do just enough to get by. | 1 2 3 4 5 6 7 | We all work to be the best and that makes us proud. |
| 6. We seldom provide each other helpful feedback. | 1 2 3 4 5 6 7 | We frequently give each other pointed and helpful feedback. |

**Total Score:**

## Commitment

| 7. We talk about each other behind our backs. | 1 2 3 4 5 6 7 | We are loyal to each other even when we are not together. |
|---|---|---|
| 8. We often belittle each others' views. | 1 2 3 4 5 6 7 | We demonstrate respect for each others' views, beliefs, and ideas. |
| 9. We withhold our points of view from each other. | 1 2 3 4 5 6 7 | We openly share our ideas even when they differ. |
| 10. We act without consideration for each other. | 1 2 3 4 5 6 7 | Before we act, we take the welfare of our teammates into consideration. |
| 11. We ignore poor performance and broken promises. | 1 2 3 4 5 6 7 | We hold one another accountable for performing to our standards. |
| 12. We undermine the development efforts of individual team members. | 1 2 3 4 5 6 7 | We support each other's professional and personal development. |
| 13. Each of us is in it for ourselves. | 1 2 3 4 5 6 7 | No one works toward personal goals at the expense of the team's goals. |

**Total Score:**

## Consistency

| 14. No one can tell where any of us stands. | 1 2 3 4 5 6 7 | We each say what we mean and mean what we say. |
|---|---|---|
| 15. None of us keeps our commitments. | 1 2 3 4 5 6 7 | Each of us follows through on our commitments 100 percent. |
| 16. Our output is uneven and unpredictable. | 1 2 3 4 5 6 7 | We deliver the same level of effort in our work 100 percent of the time. |

*Continued*

| 17. What we each do often doesn't match what we say. | 1 | 2 | 3 | 4 | 5 | 6 | 7 | We each walk our talk. |
|---|---|---|---|---|---|---|---|---|
| 18. Our positions vary depending on the person we are talking to. | 1 | 2 | 3 | 4 | 5 | 6 | 7 | Our positions are consistent with each of our espoused core values. |

**Total Score:** _____

## Trust Willingness

### Willingness to Invest

| 19. We've given no thought to our need for trust. | 1 | 2 | 3 | 4 | 5 | 6 | 7 | We each have an accurate assessment of the level of trust we intend to build within our team and why. |
|---|---|---|---|---|---|---|---|---|
| 20. We believe trust will just happen over time. | 1 | 2 | 3 | 4 | 5 | 6 | 7 | We each have an accurate assessment of what it will take to build trust. |
| 21. We are passive in our approach to building trust. | 1 | 2 | 3 | 4 | 5 | 6 | 7 | We each take active steps to build trust with our team members. |

**Total Score:** _____

### Willingness to Examine Assumptions

| 22. Our beliefs are unquestionable. | 1 | 2 | 3 | 4 | 5 | 6 | 7 | We continually challenge our own assumptions. |
|---|---|---|---|---|---|---|---|---|
| 23. We stick to our strongly held positions. | 1 | 2 | 3 | 4 | 5 | 6 | 7 | We are open to changing our points of view. |
| 24. We are suspicious of others' motives. | 1 | 2 | 3 | 4 | 5 | 6 | 7 | We give each other the benefit of the doubt. |
| 25. We avoid getting honest feedback. | 1 | 2 | 3 | 4 | 5 | 6 | 7 | We seek input and feedback from each other. |
| 26. We hide or cover up our mistakes from each other. | 1 | 2 | 3 | 4 | 5 | 6 | 7 | We freely admit when we are wrong. |
| 27. Our relationships are based on our assumptions and biases. | 1 | 2 | 3 | 4 | 5 | 6 | 7 | We harbor no prejudices about each other which negatively impact our relationships. |

**Total Score:** _____

### Willingness to Risk

| 28. We are blind to opportunities that present themselves. | 1 | 2 | 3 | 4 | 5 | 6 | 7 | We continually look for opportunities to innovate or improve. |
|---|---|---|---|---|---|---|---|---|

| 29. We always take the safest path. | 1  2  3  4  5  6  7 | We are willing to risk failure to try new things. |
|---|---|---|
| 30. Certain subjects are off-limits; we have undiscussible issues. | 1  2  3  4  5  6  7 | We have an open, honest climate; we can talk about anything. |
| 31. We tend to hoard or withhold information. | 1  2  3  4  5  6  7 | We freely share all information with each other; nothing is secret. |
| 32. We trust no decision made without our own input and influence. | 1  2  3  4  5  6  7 | Each of us is trusted to make decisions for the whole team. |
| 33. Two strikes and you're out. | 1  2  3  4  5  6  7 | We grant each other mistakes without it affecting our level of trust in each other. |
| 34. Trust goes to zero in new situations. | 1  2  3  4  5  6  7 | We readily trust each other even in new situations. |

**Total Score:**

## PART THREE: ASSESSING THE RESULTS

Enter your total score for each section in the score column and divide by the number of items in that section to obtain an average for each component that matches our 1–7 scale. Then total the three scores in each section and divide by the total number of items for that portion of the assessment to get a score for both trustworthiness and willingness to trust.

|  | Score | # of Items | Result |
|---|---|---|---|
| Capability |  | ÷ 6 |  |
| Commitment |  | ÷ 7 |  |
| Consistency |  | ÷ 5 |  |
| **Trustworthiness** |  | ÷ 18 |  |
| Willingness to invest |  | ÷ 3 |  |
| Willingness to examine assumptions |  | ÷ 6 |  |
| Willingness to risk |  | ÷ 7 |  |
| **Trust Willingness** |  | ÷ 16 |  |

*Continued*

Compare your calculated component score with your initial over-all assessment in Part One. Does your calculated component score match your initial estimate of the current level of trust? How large is the gap between the calculated score and the level of trust you want to have? Use the component scores and the suggested tools to design a strategy for building trust.

## Tool Suggestions

Consider using the following tools to help you build your trust capacity:

- Dialogue
- Purpose Hierarchy
- Interface Conflict Solving Model
- Checklist for Empowerment
- Team Agreements
- Building Consensus
- Surfacing Concerns
- Clarifying Values

# TRUST ASSESSMENT

## TEAM TO TEAM

This questionnaire is designed to build trust between teams within your organization. There are two parts to this assessment. The first part asks you to take a quick overall measure of the level of trust between the teams in question. The second part dissects trust into its six component parts and helps you assess where between-team trust is strongest and weakest. Answer all the questions carefully with both teams or departments in mind.

### PART ONE: OVERALL ASSESSMENT

On a scale of 1–7, how high is the *current level* of trust between these teams?

| Strong | | | Neutral | | | High |
|---|---|---|---|---|---|---|
| Mistrust | 1 | 2 | 3 | 4 | 5 | 6 | 7 | Trust |

On a scale of 1–7, how high does the level of trust between the two teams *need to be* to assure the achievement of their common purpose?

| Strong | | | Neutral | | | High |
|---|---|---|---|---|---|---|
| Mistrust | 1 | 2 | 3 | 4 | 5 | 6 | 7 | Trust |

### PART TWO: TRUST COMPONENT ASSESSMENT

The following questions will help you identify the domains in which the level of trust between teams is strongest and weakest. The contrasting descriptions are designed to provoke your thinking regarding trust. For each row, indicate the point on the continuum (from 1 to 7) that best describes this team relationship. A "1" indicates that the description on the left describes the relationship. A "7" means that the situation matches the description on the right. If neither provides a perfect description, use the rest of the scale to indicate where between the two extremes you think you fall. Circle your answers and calculate your totals for each element of trust.

*Continued*

## Trustworthiness

### Capability

| 1. We hide mistakes from each other. | 1 2 3 4 5 6 7 | Each team is honest with the other about what each can and cannot do. |
|---|---|---|
| 2. Neither team has the skills it will take to fulfill our missions. | 1 2 3 4 5 6 7 | Each team has the skills needed to fulfill our respective missions. |
| 3. We have no solid knowledge of each other's competence. | 1 2 3 4 5 6 7 | Each team has clearly demonstrated competence to the other. |
| 4. Neither team listens carefully to what the other team is trying to say. | 1 2 3 4 5 6 7 | Both teams listen empathically. |
| 5. Each team does just enough to get by. | 1 2 3 4 5 6 7 | Each team works to be the best. |
| 6. As teams, we seldom provide each other with useful feedback. | 1 2 3 4 5 6 7 | Each team receives frequent, pointed, and helpful feedback from the other. |

### Total Score:

### Commitment

| 7. We talk poorly of each other with others in the organization. | 1 2 3 4 5 6 7 | We show respect for each other even when the other team is not present. |
|---|---|---|
| 8. We often belittle each others' views or positions. | 1 2 3 4 5 6 7 | We demonstrate respect for each others' views or positions. |
| 9. We withhold our points of view from each other. | 1 2 3 4 5 6 7 | We openly share our ideas even when they differ. |
| 10. We act without consideration for each other. | 1 2 3 4 5 6 7 | Before we act, we take the needs of the other team into consideration. |
| 11. We acknowledge no inter-dependence with the other team. | 1 2 3 4 5 6 7 | We recognize and accept that we can not be successful without each other. |
| 12. We ignore the poor performance of the other team. | 1 2 3 4 5 6 7 | We hold one another accountable for performing to our standards. |
| 13. We undermine the success efforts of the other team. | 1 2 3 4 5 6 7 | We support each other's mission and goals. |

| 14. Each team is in it for themselves. | 1 2 3 4 5 6 7 | Neither team works toward their own goals at the expense of the other's. |

**Total Score:** _____

### Consistency

| 15. No one can tell where either team stands. | 1 2 3 4 5 6 7 | Each team says what it means and means what it says. |
| 16. Neither team keeps its commitments. | 1 2 3 4 5 6 7 | Each team follows through on its commitments 100 percent. |
| 17. Output is uneven and unpredictable for both teams. | 1 2 3 4 5 6 7 | Each team delivers the same level of effort 100 percent of the time. |
| 18. What each team does often doesn't match what it espouses. | 1 2 3 4 5 6 7 | Each team walks its talk. |
| 19. Team positions vary depending on which team member you talk to. | 1 2 3 4 5 6 7 | Team positions are clear and consistent. |

**Total Score:** _____

## Trust Willingness

### Willingness to Invest

| 20. We've given no thought to our need for mutual trust. | 1 2 3 4 5 6 7 | Each team has an accurate assessment of the level of trust we intend to build with the other team and why. |
| 21. We believe trust will just happen over time. | 1 2 3 4 5 6 7 | Each team has an accurate assessment of what it will take to build trust. |
| 22. We are passive in our approach to building trust. | 1 2 3 4 5 6 7 | Each team takes active steps to build trust with our team members. |

**Total Score:** _____

### Willingness to Examine Assumptions

| 23. Neither team is willing to question its position or beliefs. | 1 2 3 4 5 6 7 | Each team frequently questions its positions. |

*Continued*

| 24. Each team sticks to its strongly held positions. | 1 2 3 4 5 6 7 | Each team is open to changing its points of view. |
|---|---|---|
| 25. Each team is suspicious of the other's motives. | 1 2 3 4 5 6 7 | Each team gives the other the benefit of the doubt. |
| 26. We avoid getting honest feedback. | 1 2 3 4 5 6 7 | We seek input and feedback from each other. |
| 27. We hide or cover up our mistakes from each other. | 1 2 3 4 5 6 7 | We freely admit when we are wrong. |
| 28. Our relationships are based on our assumptions and biases. | 1 2 3 4 5 6 7 | We harbor no prejudices about each other which negatively impact our relationships. |

**Total Score:**

### Willingness to Risk

| 29. Each team is strongly invested in the status quo. | 1 2 3 4 5 6 7 | We continually look together for opportunities to innovate or improve. |
|---|---|---|
| 30. Each team always take the safest path. | 1 2 3 4 5 6 7 | Each team is willing to risk failure to try new things. |
| 31. Certain subjects are off-limits; we have undiscussible issues. | 1 2 3 4 5 6 7 | We have an open, honest climate; we can talk with the other team about anything. |
| 32. We tend to hoard or withhold information from each other. | 1 2 3 4 5 6 7 | We freely share all information with each other; nothing is secret. |
| 33. We trust no decision the other team makes without us. | 1 2 3 4 5 6 7 | Each of us is trusted to make decisions for both teams. |
| 34. Two strikes and they're out. | 1 2 3 4 5 6 7 | We grant each other mistakes without it affecting our level of trust in each other. |
| 35. Trust goes to zero in new situations. | 1 2 3 4 5 6 7 | We readily trust each other even in new situations. |

**Total Score:**

## PART THREE: ASSESSING THE RESULTS

Enter your total score for each section in the score column and divide by the number of items in that section to obtain an average for each component that matches our 1–7 scale. Then total the three scores in each section and divide by the total number of items for that portion of the assessment to get a score for both trustworthiness and willingness to trust.

| | Score | # of Items | Result |
|---|---|---|---|
| Capability | | ÷ 6 | |
| Commitment | | ÷ 8 | |
| Consistency | | ÷ 5 | |
| **Trustworthiness** | | ÷ 19 | |
| Willingness to invest | | ÷ 3 | |
| Willingness to examine assumptions | | ÷ 6 | |
| Willingness to risk | | ÷ 7 | |
| **Trust Willingness** | | ÷ 16 | |

Compare your calculated component score with your initial overall assessment in Part One. Does your calculated component score match your initial estimate of the current level of trust? How large is the gap between the calculated score and the level of trust you want to have? Use the component scores and the suggested tools to design a strategy for building trust.

## Tool Suggestions

Consider using the following tools to help you build your trust capacity:

- Purpose Hierarchy
- Interface Conflict Solving Model
- Team Agreements
- Building Consensus
- Surfacing Concerns
- Clarifying Values

# TRUST ASSESSMENT

## ORGANIZATION

This questionnaire is designed to help you build trust within your organization. There are two parts to this assessment. The first part asks you to take a quick overall measure of the level of trust within your organization. The second part dissects trust into its six component parts and helps you assess where organizational trust is strongest and weakest. Answer all the questions carefully with your organization and its leaders in mind.

### PART ONE: OVERALL ASSESSMENT

On a scale of 1–7, how high is the *current level* of trust within this organization?

| Strong | | | | Neutral | | | | High |
|--------|---|---|---|---------|---|---|---|------|
| Mistrust | 1 | 2 | 3 | 4 | 5 | 6 | 7 | Trust |

On a scale of 1– 7, how high does the level of trust within the organization *need to be* to assure the achievement of your mission and vision?

| Strong | | | | Neutral | | | | High |
|--------|---|---|---|---------|---|---|---|------|
| Mistrust | 1 | 2 | 3 | 4 | 5 | 6 | 7 | Trust |

### PART TWO: TRUST COMPONENT ASSESSMENT

The following questions will help you identify the domains in which the level of trust within your organization is strongest and weakest. The contrasting descriptions are designed to provoke your thinking regarding trust. For each row, indicate the point on the continuum (from 1 to 7) that best describes your organization. A "1" indicates that the description on the left describes your organization perfectly. A "7" means that your organization matches the description on the right. If neither provides a perfect description, use the rest of the scale to indicate where between the two extremes you think your organization falls. Circle your answers and calculate your totals for each element of trust. [Read "we" to mean the organization as a whole.]

## Trustworthiness

### Capability

| 1. We hire based on seniority, cost, or nepotism. | 1 | 2 | 3 | 4 | 5 | 6 | 7 | We hire for competence and talent. |
|---|---|---|---|---|---|---|---|---|
| 2. Little time or money is expended on learning. | 1 | 2 | 3 | 4 | 5 | 6 | 7 | We promote continuous learning. |
| 3. Our leaders do not demonstrate competence. | 1 | 2 | 3 | 4 | 5 | 6 | 7 | Our leaders are talented people who get results. |
| 4. People are assigned to jobs based on seniority or availability. | 1 | 2 | 3 | 4 | 5 | 6 | 7 | People are matched to jobs for which they have the skills to perform. |
| 5. We have to compensate for the incompetence of some. | 1 | 2 | 3 | 4 | 5 | 6 | 7 | Everyone pulls their own weight. |
| 6. The organization's direction is unclear or changes unpredictably. | 1 | 2 | 3 | 4 | 5 | 6 | 7 | The organization is dedicated to its clear and noble vision. |
| 7. We have significant financial or quality problems. | 1 | 2 | 3 | 4 | 5 | 6 | 7 | The organization consistently meets or exceeds its goals. |

**Total Score:** _____

### Commitment

| 8. Turnover and brain drain are high. | 1 | 2 | 3 | 4 | 5 | 6 | 7 | We do what it takes to keep good employees. |
|---|---|---|---|---|---|---|---|---|
| 9. Employees are expected to just toe the line. | 1 | 2 | 3 | 4 | 5 | 6 | 7 | Employees have a say in issues that affect them. |
| 10. Employees are expected to be seen but not heard. | 1 | 2 | 3 | 4 | 5 | 6 | 7 | The organization solicits employee input before making big changes. |
| 11. Tools and equipment are kept locked up. | 1 | 2 | 3 | 4 | 5 | 6 | 7 | People are given open access to the equipment they need to do their jobs. |
| 12. We operate on a "need to know" basis. | 1 | 2 | 3 | 4 | 5 | 6 | 7 | Business information is openly shared and made available to all. |
| 13. We hire and lay off regularly. | 1 | 2 | 3 | 4 | 5 | 6 | 7 | We have a commitment to keeping and promoting our workers. |
| 14. Work comes first; family and personal needs come second. | 1 | 2 | 3 | 4 | 5 | 6 | 7 | There is demonstrated commitment to the well-being of employees. |

**Total Score:** _____

*Continued*

## Consistency

| | | |  | | | | | |
|---|---|---|---|---|---|---|---|---|
| 15. Our business systems have little relevance to our goals or values. | 1 | 2 | 3 | 4 | 5 | 6 | 7 | Our business systems are aligned with the organization's values. |
| 16. No two people are treated the same. | 1 | 2 | 3 | 4 | 5 | 6 | 7 | We are dedicated to fair and equitable treatment. |
| 17. Discipline is arbitrarily enforced. | 1 | 2 | 3 | 4 | 5 | 6 | 7 | Consequences are clear, fair, and uniformly applied. |
| 18. Accountabilities are unclear or seldom enforced. | 1 | 2 | 3 | 4 | 5 | 6 | 7 | Accountabilities are clear and enforced. |
| 19. The organization has been known to go back on promises. | 1 | 2 | 3 | 4 | 5 | 6 | 7 | The organization keeps its word with employees and customers. |
| 20. Ethics are OK as long as they don't interfere with business. | 1 | 2 | 3 | 4 | 5 | 6 | 7 | The organization devoutly adheres to ethical business practices. |
| 21. Leaders say one thing and do another. | 1 | 2 | 3 | 4 | 5 | 6 | 7 | Leaders walk their talk. |
| 22. Mistakes are never acknowledged. | 1 | 2 | 3 | 4 | 5 | 6 | 7 | Leaders admit when they are wrong. |
| 23. Leaders have been known to go back on promises. | 1 | 2 | 3 | 4 | 5 | 6 | 7 | Leaders keep their commitments. |

**Total Score:**

## Trust Willingness

### Willingness to Invest

| | | | | | | | | |
|---|---|---|---|---|---|---|---|---|
| 24. The organization is thoughtless about building a climate of trust. | 1 | 2 | 3 | 4 | 5 | 6 | 7 | There is a common understanding of the need for trust. |
| 25. The organization assumes trust will just happen. | 1 | 2 | 3 | 4 | 5 | 6 | 7 | There is a common understanding of what it takes to build trust. |
| 26. The organization is passive in its approach to building trust. | 1 | 2 | 3 | 4 | 5 | 6 | 7 | The organization takes active steps to build a climate of trust. |

**Total Score:**

### Willingness to Examine Assumptions

| | | | | | | | | |
|---|---|---|---|---|---|---|---|---|
| 27. Organizational values, beliefs, or assumptions are never questioned. | 1 | 2 | 3 | 4 | 5 | 6 | 7 | We continually challenge our own assumptions. |
| 28. Our leaders stick to their strongly held positions. | 1 | 2 | 3 | 4 | 5 | 6 | 7 | Our leaders are open to changing their points of view. |

| | | | | | | | | |
|---|---|---|---|---|---|---|---|---|
| 29. Motives are always questioned. | 1 | 2 | 3 | 4 | 5 | 6 | 7 | We assume that people operate for the benefit of the organization. |
| 30. The organization and its leaders avoid getting honest feedback. | 1 | 2 | 3 | 4 | 5 | 6 | 7 | The organization and its leaders seek input and feedback from employees and customers. |
| 31. Mistakes are kept hidden. | 1 | 2 | 3 | 4 | 5 | 6 | 7 | Leaders freely admit when they are wrong. |
| 32. Decisions and policy reflect organizational prejudices. | 1 | 2 | 3 | 4 | 5 | 6 | 7 | The organization harbors no prejudices about employees or others with whom it does business. |

**Total Score:**

## Willingness to Risk

| | | | | | | | | |
|---|---|---|---|---|---|---|---|---|
| 33. We are blind to opportunities that present themselves. | 1 | 2 | 3 | 4 | 5 | 6 | 7 | We continually look for opportunities to innovate or improve. |
| 34. We always take the safest path. | 1 | 2 | 3 | 4 | 5 | 6 | 7 | We are willing to risk failure to try new things. |
| 35. Certain subjects are off-limits; we have undiscussible issues. | 1 | 2 | 3 | 4 | 5 | 6 | 7 | We have an open, honest climate; we can talk about anything. |
| 36. We tend to hoard or withhold information. | 1 | 2 | 3 | 4 | 5 | 6 | 7 | Information is freely shared with all employees. |
| 37. Leaders trust no decision they haven't made themselves. | 1 | 2 | 3 | 4 | 5 | 6 | 7 | Employees are empowered to make significant business decisions. |
| 38. Mistakes are punished. | 1 | 2 | 3 | 4 | 5 | 6 | 7 | Mistakes are used for learning. |
| 39. Trust goes to zero in new situations. | 1 | 2 | 3 | 4 | 5 | 6 | 7 | The organization operates on the assumption of trust even in new situations. |

**Total Score:**

## PART THREE: ASSESSING THE RESULTS

Enter your total score for each section in the score column and divide by the number of items in that section to obtain an average for each component that matches our 1–7 scale. Then total the three scores in each section and divide by the total number of items for that portion of the assessment to get a score for both trustworthiness and willingness to trust.

*Continued*

| | Score | # of Items | Result |
|---|---|---|---|
| Capability | | ÷ 7 | |
| Commitment | | ÷ 7 | |
| Consistency | | ÷ 9 | |
| **Trustworthiness** | | ÷ 23 | |
| Willingness to invest | | ÷ 3 | |
| Willingness to examine assumptions | | ÷ 6 | |
| Willingness to risk | | ÷ 7 | |
| **Trust Willingness** | | ÷ 16 | |

Compare your calculated component score with your initial overall assessment in Part One. Does your calculated component score match your initial estimate of the current level of trust? How large is the gap between the calculated score and the level of trust you want to have? Use the component scores and the suggested tools to design a strategy for building trust.

## Tool Suggestions

Consider using the following tools to help you build your trust capacity:

- Examining Organizational Practices
- Reformulating for Trust

# TRUST ASSESSMENT

## ORGANIZATION TO ORGANIZATION

This questionnaire is designed to help you build trust between your organization and another organization with whom you do business. There are two parts to this assessment. The first part asks you to take a quick overall measure of the level of trust between the organizations. The second part dissects trust into its six component parts and helps you assess where trust is strongest and weakest. Answer all the questions carefully with both organizations in mind.

### PART ONE: OVERALL ASSESSMENT

On a scale of 1–7, how high is the *current level* of trust between the organizations?

| Strong | | | | Neutral | | | | High |
|--------|---|---|---|---------|---|---|---|------|
| Mistrust | 1 | 2 | 3 | 4 | 5 | 6 | 7 | Trust |

On a scale of 1–7, how high does the level of trust between organizations *need to be* to assure the achievement of your organization's goals?

| Strong | | | | Neutral | | | | High |
|--------|---|---|---|---------|---|---|---|------|
| Mistrust | 1 | 2 | 3 | 4 | 5 | 6 | 7 | Trust |

### PART TWO: TRUST COMPONENT ASSESSMENT

The following questions will help you identify the domains in which the level of trust is strongest and weakest. The contrasting descriptions are designed to provoke your thinking regarding trust. For each row, indicate the point on the continuum (from 1 to 7) that best describes the relationship between the two organizations. A "1" indicates that the description on the left describes the relationship perfectly. A "7" means that the relationship matches the description on the right. If neither provides a perfect description, use the rest of the scale to indicate where between the two extremes you think the relationship falls. Circle your answers and calculate your totals for each element of trust.

*Continued*

## Trustworthiness

### Capability

1. We hide mistakes from each other.    1 2 3 4 5 6 7    Each organization is honest with the other about what it can and can't do.

2. Neither organization's workforce has the skills needed to fulfill our respective missions.    1 2 3 4 5 6 7    Each organization has a highly skilled workforce.

3. We have no solid knowledge of each other's competence.    1 2 3 4 5 6 7    Each organization has clearly demonstrated its competence.

4. Neither organization listens carefully to what the other says.    1 2 3 4 5 6 7    Both organizations listen empathically.

5. The quality of output is questionable on both sides.    1 2 3 4 5 6 7    Each organization sets and achieves high standards for quality.

6. Both organizations suffer from outdated technology.    1 2 3 4 5 6 7    Each organization possesses state-of-the-art technology.

7. Communication between the two organizations is cumbersome and fraught with barriers.    1 2 3 4 5 6 7    We have effective and accessible mechanisms for communicating with each other.

**Total Score:**

### Commitment

8. We talk poorly of each other when members of the other organization are not present.    1 2 3 4 5 6 7    We show respect for each other even when members of the other organization are not present.

9. There are insurmountable cultural differences between our two organizations.    1 2 3 4 5 6 7    We value and leverage the cultural differences between our two organizations.

10. We withhold points of view from each other.    1 2 3 4 5 6 7    We openly share our ideas even when they differ.

11. We act without consideration for each other.    1 2 3 4 5 6 7    Before we act, we take the needs of the other organization into account.

12. We see no interdependence with the other organization.    1 2 3 4 5 6 7    We recognize and accept that we cannot be successful without each other.

| 13. We ignore the poor performance of the other organization. | 1 | 2 | 3 | 4 | 5 | 6 | 7 | We hold one another accountable for performing to standard. |
|---|---|---|---|---|---|---|---|---|
| 14. We undermine the success efforts of the other organization. | 1 | 2 | 3 | 4 | 5 | 6 | 7 | We support each other's mission and goals. |
| 15. Each organization is in it for itself. | 1 | 2 | 3 | 4 | 5 | 6 | 7 | Neither works toward its own goals at the expense of the other's. |

**Total Score:** _____

## Consistency

| 16. No one can tell where either organization stands. | 1 | 2 | 3 | 4 | 5 | 6 | 7 | Each organization says what it means and means what it says. |
|---|---|---|---|---|---|---|---|---|
| 17. Neither organization keeps its commitments. | 1 | 2 | 3 | 4 | 5 | 6 | 7 | Each organization follows through on its commitments 100 percent. |
| 18. Output is unreliable for both organizations. | 1 | 2 | 3 | 4 | 5 | 6 | 7 | Each organization delivers the same level of effort 100 percent of the time. |
| 19. Neither organization walks its talk. | 1 | 2 | 3 | 4 | 5 | 6 | 7 | Each organization walks its talk. |
| 20. The positions of the organizations vary depending on which representative you talk to. | 1 | 2 | 3 | 4 | 5 | 6 | 7 | Organization positions are clear and consistent. |

**Total Score:** _____

# Trust Willingness

## Willingness to Invest

| 21. We've given no thought to our need for mutual trust. | 1 | 2 | 3 | 4 | 5 | 6 | 7 | Each organization has an accurate assessment of the level of trust we intend to build with the other and why. |
|---|---|---|---|---|---|---|---|---|
| 22. We believe trust will just happen over time. | 1 | 2 | 3 | 4 | 5 | 6 | 7 | Each organization has an accurate assessment of what it will take to build trust between the two entities. |
| 23. We are passive in our approach to building trust. | 1 | 2 | 3 | 4 | 5 | 6 | 7 | Each organization takes active steps to build trust in the relationship. |

**Total Score:** _____

*Continued*

## Willingness to Examine Assumptions

| | | | | | | | | |
|---|---|---|---|---|---|---|---|---|
| 24. Neither organization is willing to question its position or beliefs. | 1 | 2 | 3 | 4 | 5 | 6 | 7 | Each organization frequently questions its positions. |
| 25. Each organization sticks to its strongly held positions. | 1 | 2 | 3 | 4 | 5 | 6 | 7 | Each organization is open to changing its points of view. |
| 26. Each organization is suspicious of the other's motives. | 1 | 2 | 3 | 4 | 5 | 6 | 7 | Each organization gives the other the benefit of the doubt. |
| 27. We avoid getting honest feedback. | 1 | 2 | 3 | 4 | 5 | 6 | 7 | We seek input and feedback from each other. |
| 28. We hide or cover up our mistakes from each other. | 1 | 2 | 3 | 4 | 5 | 6 | 7 | We freely admit when we are wrong. |
| 29. Our relationship is based on our assumptions and biases. | 1 | 2 | 3 | 4 | 5 | 6 | 7 | We harbor no prejudices about each other that negatively impact our relationship. |

### Total Score:

## Willingness to Risk

| | | | | | | | | |
|---|---|---|---|---|---|---|---|---|
| 30. Each organization is strongly invested in the status quo. | 1 | 2 | 3 | 4 | 5 | 6 | 7 | We continually look together for opportunities to innovate or improve. |
| 31. Each organization always takes the safest path. | 1 | 2 | 3 | 4 | 5 | 6 | 7 | Each organization is willing to risk failure to try new things. |
| 32. Certain subjects are off-limits; we have undiscussible issues. | 1 | 2 | 3 | 4 | 5 | 6 | 7 | We have an open, honest climate; we can talk with the other organization about anything. |
| 33. We tend to hoard or withhold information from each other. | 1 | 2 | 3 | 4 | 5 | 6 | 7 | We freely share all information with each other; nothing is secret. |
| 34. We trust no decision the other organization makes without us. | 1 | 2 | 3 | 4 | 5 | 6 | 7 | Each of us is trusted to make decisions for both organizations. |
| 35. Two strikes and they're out. | 1 | 2 | 3 | 4 | 5 | 6 | 7 | We grant each other mistakes without it affecting our level of trust in each other. |
| 36. Trust goes to zero in new situations. | 1 | 2 | 3 | 4 | 5 | 6 | 7 | We readily trust each other even in new situations. |

### Total Score:

## PART THREE: ASSESSING THE RESULTS

Enter your total score for each section in the score column and divide by the number of items in that section to obtain an average for each component that matches our 1–7 scale. Then total the three scores in each section and divide by the total number of items for that portion of the assessment to get a score for both trustworthiness and willingness to trust.

| | Score | # of Items | Result |
|---|---|---|---|
| Capability | | ÷ 7 | |
| Commitment | | ÷ 8 | |
| Consistency | | ÷ 5 | |
| **Trustworthiness** | | ÷ 20 | |
| Willingness to invest | | ÷ 3 | |
| Willingness to examine assumptions | | ÷ 6 | |
| Willingness to risk | | ÷ 7 | |
| **Trust Willingness** | | ÷ 16 | |

Compare your calculated component score with your initial overall assessment in Part One. Does your calculated component score match your initial estimate of the current level of trust? How large is the gap between the calculated score and the level of trust you want to have? Use the component scores and the suggested tools to design a strategy for building trust.

### Tool Suggestions

Consider using the following tools to help you build your trust capacity:

- Purpose Hierarchy
- Interface Conflict Solving Model
- Team Agreements
- Building Consensus
- Surfacing Concerns
- Clarifying Values

*Continued*

# Appendix B

# Tools for Trust

## USING THE TOOLS FOR TRUST

This appendix contains a collection of tools designed to build trust in varying types of situations and relationships. It represents neither an exhaustive nor comprehensive set of tools, but rather a starter set of activities upon which you may draw to begin your journey toward trust. The tools are linked to the various trust assessments to enable you to pinpoint the specific deficiencies in each of your relationships of concern.

### Where to Start

We suggest beginning by selecting a particular level or relationship you would like to work on (for example, your own trust performance, or a relationship with another, within a team, between teams, or across a whole organization). Take the assessment that is directed at that level and then select a tool from among the list of tools at the end of that assessment to target your trust-building efforts. Each tool included in this appendix has four parts. The first two parts name the level and component for easy reference. The third section provides a brief description of the tool and its intent. The fourth section provides detailed instructions for applying the tool to your situation.

On the following page is a summary list of the tools that identifies the level and the specific component of trust (consistency, commitment, capability, willingness to invest, examine assumptions, and risk-taking) each addresses.

| Tool | Level | Component |
|---|---|---|
| Conceptual Image Document | Self | Willingness to examine assumptions<br>Willingness to risk |
| Personal Life Plan | Self | Willingness to invest<br>Willingness to risk |
| Key Relationship and Trust | Interpersonal | Willingness to invest |
| Ladder of Inference | Self<br>Interpersonal | Willingness to examine assumptions |
| Uncovering Assumptions That Block Trust | Self<br>Interpersonal | Willingness to examine assumptions |
| Finding Common Ground | Interpersonal<br>Within team<br>Between team | Commitment |
| Dialogues That Build Trust | Interpersonal<br>Within team | Willingness to examine assumptions |
| Enhancing Team Trust | Within team | Willingness to examine assumptions<br>Consistency<br>Commitment<br>Capability |
| Creating Trust Through Empowerment | Within team | Commitment<br>Capability |
| Revealing Concerns That Block Trust | Interpersonal<br>Within team | Willingness to examine assumptions |
| Developing Optimal Trust Relations | Interpersonal<br>Within team | Commitment<br>Capability |
| Building Trust by Building Consensus | Within team<br>Between team | Commitment<br>Capability |
| Clarifying Trust Values | Within team<br>Between team<br>Institutional | Commitment |
| Retooling for Organization Trust | Institutional | Willingness to invest<br>Willingness to examine assumptions<br>Willingness to risk |
| Reformulating for Trust | Institutional | Willingness to risk |

# CONCEPTUAL IMAGE DOCUMENT

| | |
|---|---|
| **Level:** | **Self** |
| **Component:** | **Willingness to examine assumptions and willingness to risk** |

## Description

The Conceptual Image Document provides structure for self-discovery. The CID poses a series of questions, arranged in four parts, which allow for long-term reflection and a review of supportive short-term goals/actions. The thrust of the reflection is to bring to consciousness a purpose for being and to seek consistency of near-term actions. The understanding of our life's purpose provides perspective for our daily living. Our unique insight into our individual life's purpose provides strength and direction.

Such a process is important because when we are clear about our purpose in life, others increase their trust in us. People know where we are coming from with our words and actions. They begin to see the uniformity between our direction in life and our actions. We are more dependable and reliable when we make commitments because the commitments are in order with our reason for being. An internal integrity forms. In both subtle and bold ways this internal integrity is conveyed to those around us.

## How to Use

This document is designed for individual use. It consists of four general areas containing thought-provoking questions. It is not an evaluation tool; it is an individual improvement tool. It is intended to spark introspection, consciousness, and personal direction setting. Your conceptual image document is dynamic. Consider your first draft to be version 1.0, to be periodically updated as you progress through life.

1. Conceptual image of yourself, both personal and professional

    • Who are you?

    • What do you do? Who do you do it with? What value do you add to your customers? To your organization? To the world?

    • How do you introduce yourself? Who do you say you are to others?

- What are your personal strengths? Why? What are your technical and professional competencies?

- What are your weaknesses? Why?

- What do you have passion for? What gives you joy?

- Who do you learn from? What are you learning from them? Are you a mentor to anyone? If so, to who and concerning what area?

- How well do you manage the agreements you make with others and yourself? How do you manage trust with others? How trustworthy are you?

- What are your core values? What operating principles for daily living have you derived from these values?

- What results are you producing? Why? How do you achieve results? What is your approach when results are not forthcoming?

2. Purpose, personal and professional vision

   - What is your life's purpose? Why are you here?

   - If your life were on tape, and you fast-forwarded the tape so that you were at the end looking back, what would you see? How would you feel?

   - What in your past would you change?

3. Goals and objectives (2–5 years), both personal and professional

   - What are your goals and objectives?

   - What areas in your life do these goals and objectives encompass? What areas are not addressed?

   - How would you know if these goals and objectives were accomplished?

4. Near term actions (3–6 months)

   - What actions will you take to improve yourself personally and professionally? What results do you expect to create in the next 3–6 months—

     - to fulfill your life's purpose?

     - to move toward your vision?

     - to move toward your goals and objectives?

   - What will you experiment with? What risks will you take?

- What will you—
  - read?
  - do?
  - study?
  - experience?
- What feedback will you seek?
- What relationships will you create, mend, or improve?
- How will you build agreements and trust?

# PERSONAL LIFE PLAN

| | |
|---|---|
| **Level:** | **Self** |
| **Component:** | **Willingness to invest and willingness to risk** |

## Description

The Life Plan is both a document and process, which connects our daily activities with our deeper understanding of what gives meaning to our lives. Creating a Life Plan helps us define our personal goals and aspirations: what we want to create of ourselves and in the world around us.

There is a great deal of power in having both a personal vision and a clear picture of our current reality. Having this perspective will generate a force within us that will move us toward our vision and the production of tangible results.

It has been our experience that people often hesitate to take the first step in developing a Life Plan. One reason is that many people believe that the document must be perfect and complete. Quite the opposite is intended. The Life Plan is a lifelong working document. Begin with an imperfect first version knowing that you will enhance it over time. The key is to start.

The Life Plan is intended to be a living document. We suggest you revisit your Life Plan about once every year, and perhaps more frequently in times of personal change. Many people prefer to reexamine their Life Plan near their birthdays.

## How to Use

1. Begin by identifying the significant events in your life. A significant life event is a specific happening—a critical incident—a key episode in your past, set in a particular time and place. It is a specific moment in your life that stands out to you for some reason. Describe several of the most critical incidents in your life to date. What was the impact of these events on the course of your life and who you are as a person?

2. Next examine what gives you joy in your life. Under what circumstances do you experience the feeling of joy?

3. Step three involves identifying your core values. Core values need no rational or external justification, nor do they sway with trends and fads of the day. Principles are self-evident guidelines for human conduct, basic truths. What are your personal core values? Which principles are most important to you? What values and principles do you live by?

4. Use the answers you provided to steps 1–3 to craft a purpose statement for your life. What is your purpose for being?

5. Now craft an image of yourself in the near future. When you fast-forward your life's videotape five years ahead, what do you see? Who are you and how are you engaged in life?

## Planning the Parts of the Whole

In this section, seven areas of life are offered. However, other areas can be added or substituted in order to better fit your mental breakdown of your life's major areas. Within each area, you are asked to describe a future vision (or point of arrival), a current state (or point of departure), and the actions required to achieve your vision. For each area in which you want to focus, establish one or more specific, measurable goals and outline your current performance related to these goals.

As you complete this section, don't feel pressured to sign up for aggressive goals in each area. While it can be appealing and seductive to set aggressive goals, try to focus on what is realistic for you. Most of us have experienced disappointment in the area of goal setting—unmet New Year's resolutions are a common example. Our suggestion is to focus your goals on three to five areas. Consider the option of merely maintaining and monitoring other areas in which you've chosen not to focus.

If you're struggling with which projects to take on, please stop for a minute, and review your work in earlier sections. Reread your life's purpose, your principles, your values, and so on. Trust these core areas to guide you in this planning process.

## Conditions for Success

What are the conditions internal to you that you need in order to succeed in the areas you have declared (for example, state of mind, state of being, approaches to life, personal skills, and so on)? What are the conditions external to you that you need in order to succeed (for example, family, support, and so on)?

**Spiritual**

| Point of arrival: | Point of departure: |
|---|---|
| Specific measurable goals:<br>1.<br><br>2. | Current results:<br>1.<br><br>2. |

**Family**

| Point of arrival: | Point of departure: |
|---|---|
| Specific measurable goals:<br>1.<br><br>2. | Current results:<br>1.<br><br>2. |

**Intellectual Growth**

| Point of arrival: | Point of departure: |
|---|---|
| Specific measurable goals:<br>1.<br><br>2. | Current results:<br>1.<br><br>2. |

**Physical**

| Point of arrival: | Point of departure: |
|---|---|
| Specific measurable goals:<br>1.<br><br>2. | Current results:<br>1.<br><br>2. |

**Vocation**

| Point of arrival: | Point of departure: |
|---|---|
| Specific measurable goals:<br>1.<br><br>2. | Current results:<br>1.<br><br>2. |

**Financial**

| Point of arrival: | Point of departure: |
|---|---|
| Specific measurable goals:<br>1.<br><br>2. | Current results:<br>1.<br><br>2. |

**Community**

| Point of arrival: | Point of departure: |
|---|---|
| Specific measurable goals:<br>1.<br><br>2. | Current results:<br>1.<br><br>2. |

# KEY RELATIONSHIPS AND TRUST

**Level:** **Interpersonal**

**Component:** **Willingness to invest**

## Description

This tool is designed to help you become aware of the level of trust in the relationships that matter to you and to become intentional in building trust in the relationships that need it.

## How to Use

Think of the people with whom you want a trusting relationship. They might be work relationships or personal relationships. Write the names of these people on the worksheet provided on page 116. The worksheet provides space for five names, but feel free to include as many as necessary.

In the first column to the right of the name assess the current level of trust you have with each person on a scale from 1 to 10, 10 being high. Then assess the level of trust you think *should* exist between you and each of those people.

Once you become aware of the gap (if any) that exists in the level of trust in each relationship, think about the steps you are willing to take to grow trust in that relationship. Remember the basic strategies at your disposal: developing your own willingness to examine your assumptions and take a risk with that person, as well as building your own trustworthiness. Use the space provided below each name to record your ideas.

| | Current level of trust | Desired level of trust |
|---|---|---|
| Name: | | |
| Steps I will take: | | |
| Name: | | |
| Steps I will take: | | |
| Name: | | |
| Steps I will take: | | |
| Name: | | |
| Steps I will take: | | |
| Name: | | |
| Steps I will take: | | |

# LADDER OF INFERENCE

**Level:** **Self and interpersonal**

**Component:** **Willingness to examine assumptions**

## Description

The Ladder of Inference, developed by Chris Argyris of MIT, is a particularly effective tool for revealing and examining the assumptions on which we base our beliefs and values. The tool uses the metaphor of the ladder to illustrate the path our minds take to turn experiences into abstract conclusions or beliefs. Most of the time (or so we'd like to think) the path is rational and the conclusions appropriate. Our trust is so high in our unconscious process that we begin to operate on those conclusions as if they were absolute truth. Understanding the ladder and using it to work backwards—that is climb back down our mental path—can help determine whether the assumptions that affect your ability to trust are appropriate and helpful.

## How to Use

Figure B.1 illustrates the ladder and each of the steps in our mental process. Use the steps of the ladder to examine your beliefs to become aware of your own thinking, make your reasoning explicit for others, or to help someone else examine their own assumptions.

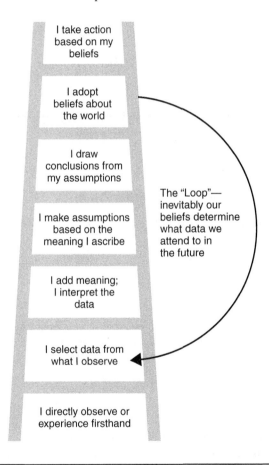

**Figure B.1**　Ladder of inference.

*Source:* From *The Fifth Discipline* by Peter M. Senge, copyright ©1990 by Peter M. Senge. Used by permission of Doubleday, a division of Random House, Inc.

These questions may help you make best use of the ladder:

- What was the observable data behind my conclusion?

- Does everyone see that data the same way I do?

- What leap did I make to turn that data into a conclusion?

## For More Information:

Argyris, C. *Reasoning, Learning, and Action.* San Francisco: Jossey-Bass, 1982.

————. *Overcoming Organizational Defenses.* Needham, MA: Allyn and Bacon, 1990.

Senge, P., et al. *The Fifth Discipline Fieldbook.* New York: Doubleday, 1994.

# UNCOVERING ASSUMPTIONS THAT BLOCK TRUST

| | |
|---|---|
| **Level:** | **Self and interpersonal** |
| **Component:** | **Willingness to examine assumptions** |

## Description

This exercise, based on one designed by Chris Argyris of MIT, is another excellent tool for revealing and examining the assumptions that block our ability to move forward with trust. It may work best as a complement to Name Your Concerns.

## How to Use

Begin by choosing a troublesome situation or relationship; one where trust building seems blocked. Recollect one or two conversations or events that typify the situation for you. Divide a piece of paper into two columns. Label the left-hand column "What I was thinking" and the right-hand column "What was actually said" (Figure B.2).

In the right-hand column write out one of the conversations you have had with the person in question. If you cannot recall one, feel free to create a conversation that you think you *would* have if you tried to talk about your issues.

| What I was thinking | What was said |
|---|---|

**Figure B.2**   Unspoken assumptions.

In the left-hand column write your thoughts or feelings associated with each part of the conversation. You know, the comments or beliefs that you censored out of the conversation.

Use the document you have created to examine your assumptions and beliefs about the person or the situation. Use the questions that follow to help you make sense of your own thinking:

- What has lead me to think this way?

- What are the assumptions that have led to these conclusions?

- What am I getting out of holding these beliefs?

- What is this thinking costing me?

- How do I contribute to what is going wrong?

- Why didn't I say what I was thinking?

- How would I have liked the conversation to have gone?

- What will I do differently next time I am in the situation?

## For More Information:

Argyris, C. *Theory in Practice*. San Francisco: Jossey-Bass, 1974.
Senge, P., et al. *The Fifth Discipline Fieldbook*. New York: Doubleday, 1994.

# FINDING COMMON GROUND

| | |
|---|---|
| **Level:** | **Interpersonal, within team, and between teams** |
| **Component:** | **Commitment** |

## Description

This approach to finding common ground uses a strategy called a "purpose hierarchy." A purpose hierarchy links the hows to whys. For any effort, there is a hierarchy of reasons for doing something. For example, you improve quality which improves customer satisfaction, which improves market share, which enlarges the impact on the community, which makes a better world. People may often disagree on the how, but if you can get them to agree on a higher purpose, they will work in alignment instead of spending their energies fighting one another. This tool also helps people understand how their piece fits into the larger work of the organization.

## How to Use

To create a purpose hierarchy, begin by asking "Why?" For example, if you are using a purpose hierarchy to create a team mission, ask, "Why do we exist?" Write the answer in the middle of a flip chart. Then keep asking why, writing team members' answers on higher and higher lines. To go the opposite direction, ask, "How might we do this?" Working down the chart should generate action items or goals that are aligned with the purpose. Figure B.3 shows an example for a fast-food restaurant that is trying to "develop healthier fast foods."

**Figure B.3** Purpose hierarchy.

# DIALOGUES THAT BUILD TRUST

**Level:** **Interpersonal or within team**

**Component:** **Willingness to examine assumptions**

## Description

A dialogue is a way of exchanging ideas that differs significantly from a discussion. The purpose of a discussion is to present and defend a particular idea or position in preparation for making a decision. A dialogue, on the other hand, is the free and creative exploration of ideas that requires suspending our own views and listening deeply to others. The purpose of a dialogue is to invent as many ways as possible to make all the positions of the participants correct and valid at the same time. Discussion is necessary to decision making and action. Dialoguing is better for learning and innovating. In our action-oriented culture it is not surprising that we are very adept at discussion and sadly inexperienced in dialoguing.

Dialoguing as a creative strategy allows people to gain new insights and reach innovative conclusions that participants would unlikely reach on their own. It is a useful tool whenever your group is trying to creatively solve a tough problem or when people begin to argue over whose position is right.

Dialoguing is only feasible if trust is high and authority and hierarchy are absent. It requires recognizing our assumptions, distinguishing them from those thoughts or beliefs actually based on facts, and then holding them up for critical public examination.

## How to Use

To facilitate a dialogue you must assure that everyone involved understands the principles and ground rules. Begin by reviewing and clarifying the assumptions listed below:

- Everyone has equal opportunity to speak

- No speaker may be interrupted

- Everyone will make the commitment to listen attentively

- Everyone must agree to accept whatever is said as true and correct without argument or disagreement

Record the major points of each person's perspective on a chart. When everyone has had a chance to share their ideas, try to invent as many new solutions or innovations that incorporate as many of the views as possible. The point is not to find the "right" idea or solution, but to see if anything new can be generated by mixing the ideas presented.

# ENHANCING TEAM TRUST

| | |
|---|---|
| **Level:** | **Within team** |
| **Component:** | **Willingness to examine assumptions; and build commitment, capability, and consistency** |

## Description

Early in its formation, a team should lay the foundation for a productive relationship by developing team agreements—a set of ground rules that govern behavior in the team. This often means postponing what the team will consider its "real work" to spend time discussing "process"—how the team will work together. However, taking this time will help the team reveal assumptions about what's okay and not okay to do in a team and mutually agreeable standards for behavior.

The rules should be an expression of how people like to be treated and how they like to work together. Examples of common team agreements include "start and stop on time," "evaluate the idea, not the person," and "decisions will be made by consensus."

- Write agreements that cover procedural issues (such as "publish an agenda at least one day in advance") and interpersonal issues (such as "respect differences of opinion").

- Team agreements should be mutually agreed upon and not merely the reflection of the majority's feelings.

- They should not be cast in concrete. They should be revisited regularly to ensure that they still reflect the needs and feelings of the group.

- They should be followed by everyone. When team members violate one of the rules, they should gently be reminded of the team agreements. If the group is consistently unable to adhere to them, then the team agreements should be reexamined to ensure that they accurately reflect what the team wants and needs.

## How to Use

Create a set of plausible problem scenarios. (Use the sample set to start and add any that fit your team situation more closely.) If you have more than five people on your team, divide them into groups of three to five and give each group a set of scenario cards. Ask them to read through the cards one by one. For each card they should answer the question set following, making note of their responses.

- What agreement would we need to make to prevent this from happening?

- If this *should* happen, how could we best handle it?

When the groups have finished processing the cards (or when you feel enough time has passed), ask the groups to share the ideas they had for agreements. Post the ideas as they are shared. Let the group consider the full list and then determine if there is anything on the list that needs clarification or revision, if there is anything that is missing that should be added, or if there is anything on the list that someone cannot agree to.

Use the list as the starting point for your team agreements. Check the list from time to time to ensure that it remains relevant. As you get good at keeping them, some items may be removed. As other situations arise in the team, you may find it necessary to make new agreements and add them to the list.

## Sample Scenarios

Your team meetings never start or end on time.

Your team never sticks to the agendas prepared for the meetings.

One person always dominates your meeting time.

The same two people seem to do all the work on the team.

Your team finally made a decision on a tough issue, but one person is bad-mouthing the choice to others outside of the team.

Everyone agreed to abide by a group decision in your last meeting, but now you find a couple of members are not living up to their agreements.

A couple of people on your team are usually silent when asked for input, but love to complain after a decision has been made.

One person on your team is a real naysayer. Every time someone offers a new idea, he is always ready with a "that won't work because . . ." response.

Decisions seem to never stick with your group. Soon after a decision is made, someone always finds a reason to "revisit" it.

It seems that no matter what the issue, your team divides into two irreconcilable camps.

There are a couple of prima donnas on the team who show little respect for the ideas of other team members whom they consider less "professional."

Your team has fallen into an unsatisfying but efficient decision-making process: the loudest one (or most powerful, most stubborn, or most whatever) makes the decision.

Some people on the team carry old baggage of past offenses into every discussion. They make every decision into an opportunity for retribution.

A couple of people on your team never read the e-mails or memos sent to them.

You feel like deals get cut behind the scenes with little input or involvement of team members.

The same people get all the plum assignments.

# CREATING TRUST THROUGH EMPOWERMENT

---

**Level:**        **Within team**

**Component: Commitment and capability**

---

## Description

Empowering people with responsibility is a great way to both demonstrate your willingness to trust as well as create opportunities for others to demonstrate their trustworthiness. Empowerment works best, however, when the responsibilities being bestowed are clear and meaningful.

## How to Use

Whether you are the person with the authority to empower or you are the party seeking the additional responsibility, begin by selecting a responsibility you think is a good starting place and build a case for why transferring authority for that responsibility will benefit all parties. We've included, at the end of this exercise, a sample list of responsibilities organizations frequently use to begin the empowerment process for employees.

Use the following steps to guide your empowerment process:

1. *Define the task/responsibility.* You need to do more than name a job to assure everyone has the same understanding and expectations about it. Think through with whomever is accepting the new responsibility all that is entailed in that task. Use the following questions to help your conversation:

- What is the task?

- What are the critical steps involved in the task?

- Are there any special formats or standardized procedures that should be followed?

- Who is affected by this task and what are their needs/requirements?

- How often should this task be performed?

- Where should the "results" (if there are any tangible outputs like reports) of this task be kept or sent?

- What standards of excellence should we establish? (What would a good job look like?)

- What authority is needed to complete this task?

- What are the boundaries? (What's OK to do and what's not OK to do?)

2. *Determine preparatory needs.* Once you know what the task is, think about the best way for someone to learn how to do it. Design some activities that will allow them the opportunity to practice doing it before they "go live" and have to do it for real.

You should also consider how the learning/training will occur. Is the person who "owns" the responsibility now the best person to teach how to do it? Would it be more effective or efficient to use formal training? How soon can the training take place and how long will it be before the new owner is ready to officially take on the task?

3. *Establish a schedule.* With some tasks the handoff will be quick and all at once. Where capability is an issue, you may want to ease the new person into the task to build confidence in both parties. Consider these five options below for a gradual handoff:

- *Watch me*—the new owner of the task watches the pro or provides input (this may be part of the training).

- *Do it together*—both parties do the task together, sharing the responsibility and control.

- *You try*—the new person does the job, but under the experienced person's supervision.

- *Let me check it*—the new person performs the task, but the end product is reviewed before it "goes out the door."

- *Go for it*—immediate transfer.

Whatever your schedule, you will need to clarify the boundaries of authority that go with the task as well as review the consequences that are connected with the results (good and bad). Don't set someone up with any false assumptions or you both may get some rude surprises.

4. *Resolve concerns.* Empowerment will only work if both sides have the opportunity to share and address any concerns they may be harboring. The person with the authority to empower should ask: "Is there anything that worries me about handing off this responsibility? What would the other person need to do to allay my fears?" The concerns should be made

explicit so that the person being empowered has a chance to understand and possibly respond. Similarly, those taking on new authorities should ask themselves: "Is there anything that worries us about taking on this responsibility? What can the other person do to make us more comfortable and confident about taking on the job?" This last step rounds out the negotiation process and ensures that empowerment is handled responsibly and with success for everyone in mind.

See "Revealing Concerns That Block Trust" for more tips on how to do this last step.

### Sample list of responsibilities for organizations

| Responsibility | Responsibility | Responsibility |
|---|---|---|
| **Setting Goals**<br>Write business plan<br>Set team goals<br>Set individual goals<br>Draft budget<br>Approve purchase requests<br>Select new equipment/ tools | **Managing Work**<br>Schedule work<br>Manage priorities<br>Promote safe work practices<br>Monitor quality<br>Schedule time off/ vacations<br>Approve time off/ vacations<br>Monitor attendance | **Rewarding Results**<br>Give verbal praise<br>Offer non-monetary rewards<br>Decide on monetary rewards<br>Determine pay level of team |
| **Staffing Positions**<br>Assign work on daily basis<br>Establish criteria for hiring<br>Interview job candidates<br>Hire new employees<br>Orient new members<br>Select team leader<br>Decide on promotions<br>Remove team members<br>Terminate employees | **Coaching Performance**<br>Establish job expectations<br>Monitor performance<br>Provide informal feedback<br>Appraise team members<br>Appraise manager<br>Provide on-the-job training<br>Define training needs<br>Schedule training<br>Reinforce training<br>Support troubled employees<br>Resolve performance problems<br>Offer career guidance | **Linking to Others**<br>Propose ideas to management<br>Interact with "customers"<br>Interact with "suppliers"<br>Coordinate with other departments<br>Communicate with managers |

# REVEALING CONCERNS
# THAT BLOCK TRUST

---

**Level:**        **Interpersonal and within teams**

**Component:  Willingness to examine assumptions**

---

## Description

Sometimes the easiest way to move forward with trust is to be explicit about what is holding us back. Honest conversations in and of themselves are powerful trust-building tools. In particular, honest conversations about the roots of our mistrust give all parties the data they need to take corrective action. This tool is designed to help you clarify for yourself the concerns that are limiting your willingness to trust and to choose an approach and the words to raise them with your partner.

## How to Use

Use the following category list to help you identify and articulate your concerns about trusting in your given situation.

- I have assumptions/expectations about what will happen.

- I am worried about risking _____.

- I perceive the cost of trusting to be too high related to the benefit I will derive.

- I have doubts about the other person's ability to do the job.

- I have doubts about the other person's commitment to me or to our common goal.

When sharing your concerns be careful not to use language or an approach that will make the other person feel defensive. Begin your conversation by describing how you feel or what you fear. Give the other person a chance to respond. Be patient if they react defensively at first. Resist the urge to follow suit. Once the person has responded to your concern, ask if they have any idea what might be done to resolve your concerns. Let them identify solutions first even if you have ideas yourself. There is a chance they will hit on your idea and own it as if it were their own. If not, raise your idea by posing it as a question: What do you think of [idea]? or Would there be a problem if we [idea]?

Before you end the conversation, be sure and give the other person a chance to express any concerns they may have as well. Offer ideas about how to resolve the concern and then check to see if they had something else in mind.

# DEVELOPING OPTIMAL TRUST RELATIONSHIPS

**Level:**       **Interpersonal and within team**

**Component:  Commitment and capability**

## Description

If the past is fraught with bad, painful experiences, a trained mediator can help individuals or groups work through them to build more positive future relationships. One good model for doing this is Blake and Mouton's "Interface Conflict-Solving Model."

## How to Use

After identifying who is on which side, follow these steps that alternate between the sides doing tasks alone and together:

1. Each side describes the optimal relationship.

2. The sides share and consolidate their ideas.

3. Each side describes the actual, current relationship.

4. The sides share and consolidate.

5. Jointly, the sides plan and contract for change.

6. After a period of time, a progress review is held.

Focusing on the optimal first is an important psychological component to this process.

## For More Information

Blake, R., and J. Mouton. *Solving Costly Organizational Conflicts: Achieving Intergroup Trust, Cooperation and Teamwork.* San Francisco: Jossey-Bass, 1984.

# BUILDING TRUST BY BUILDING CONSENSUS

| | |
|---|---|
| **Level:** | **Within team or between teams** |
| **Component:** | **Commitment and capability** |

## Description

For those situations where consensus is necessary and appropriate, you will need a process that assures you reach your desired outcome without negative effects on relationships.

## How to Use

Our experience has taught us that there are five critical steps in a consensus-building process. Feel free to modify each step to suit your team's circumstances, but beware of skipping any steps. It will only come back to haunt you in the end.

1. *Determine the deadline and boundaries.* Begin by clarifying the parameters or constraints of your decision. When does reason (or outside pressures) tell you the decision *must* be made? What are your deadlines? How much time do you need to allow for a thorough process, and how will you schedule your time so that you reach a satisfying outcome? What are the non-negotiable boundaries or conditions within which the decision must be made? Are there budget constraints, contractual obligations, legal requirements, and so on, that must be honored?

2. *Determine stakeholder needs.* Next, identify all those who will be affected by the decision and determine what each party needs out of the decision. What are the needs of your customers, your organization, as well as the individual members of your team? What *must* be satisfied in order to achieve a successful decision?

3. *Gather data.* Become as educated as necessary about the issue to assure the best outcome. What information do you need before you can make an informed decision? Have the needs of all stakeholders been presented? Are there some assumptions that you need to test before you proceed?

4. *Identify the options.* Only now should you begin discussing the alternatives. Most teams make the mistake of starting with this step and end up in endless haggling or with erroneous conclusions. Consider your full range of options (beyond the favored ones you came in with). How well does each option meet the full set of needs generated in the previous conversation?

5. *Plan for action.* The work doesn't end with the decision. Be sure to plan your follow-through. How will you implement your decision? Who else needs to know about it? Do you need a fallback position? How will you know your decision was a good one? Do you need to revisit the decision? If so, when and under what circumstances?

## Tools for Reaching Consensus

The steps provide a process but may not be enough to keep you from getting stuck in endless debate or analysis–paralysis. The following are tools you may find useful in moving your consensus process along.

**The 5 Whys.** (Especially useful for step 2 of our process.) Too often groups begin their decision process by debating various solution options. The energy in this approach is focused on trying to convince, sell, and change minds. Sometimes it works, but more often it creates win/lose situations or complete deadlock. Begin instead by asking people to explain the need that they are trying to meet. Discourage them from rationalizing their solution idea by asking them "why" they hold the position they do. What need does their idea meet or what problem does it solve for them? Sometimes you must ask why several times to get at the heart of the need. (The Japanese believe it takes asking why at least five times before the core of an issue is uncovered.) Do the same for the team as a whole. Ask what common purpose the decision must serve.

**Interrelationship Digraph.** (Useful for step 3.) Sometimes before you can intelligently talk about solutions, you must have a good understanding of the problem. Use an interrelationship digraph to help sort out symptoms from causes in your problem analysis. Follow these steps to identify the critical few root causes:

1. Write a question on a board or flip chart that represents the problem you are analyzing: What problems are we currently experiencing (or are anticipating in the near term) that our solution or decision must resolve?

2. Have the participants write their answers on adhesive-backed notes, one answer per note.

3. Pick one person's note to put up on the chart and then ask for any other notes with similar or related answers. Stack the similar answers on top of each other with a summarizing label on top (for example, "lack of trust" might summarize many of the individual answers).

4. Repeat the previous step to get one more stack of similar answers.

5. With only two sets of answers on the board, draw an arrow between them indicating which primarily leads to the other. Draw the arrow from the cause to the effect. Do not draw arrows both ways!

6. Add another set of answers and consider whether there is a relationship among the three sets of answers. Draw arrows as appropriate.

7. Continue this process until all the answers are on the board, making sure that each time you add a set of answers, you consider its relationship to all the other answers on the board. Using different colored pens can help in interpreting the inevitably messy chart.

If after discussing the directions of the arrows, the participants still disagree which way they should be drawn (which is a cause or effect?), you should validate your assumptions with others before finalizing the chart.

8. When all the arrows have been drawn, count the number of arrows coming in and out of each set of answers. Those with the largest number of arrows coming out are the key causes. Problem solving will have greater impact if it addresses the causes rather than the effects. Figure B.4 shows an example of an interrelationship digraph.

**Brainstorming.** (Useful for step 4 of our process.) Brainstorming is a well-known method of generating creative ideas. To be successful, you must separate the creative process from the analytical one. If people start

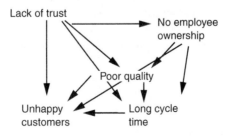

**Figure B.4** Example interrelationship digraph.

commenting on ideas as they are being generated ("That'll never work") then the creative process will stop.

There are variations on brainstorming. In addition to the free-for-all most people are familiar with, you can also go around the room, having each person give an idea. (This creates more balanced participation.) You can also give people some quiet time to think before talking, which helps the more deliberate team members contribute.

A popular variation is to use adhesive-backed notes that are assembled into affinity diagrams. Everyone writes ideas on the stickies, one idea per note. Then these are posted anonymously and organized into categories before analysis. Using this type of process separates the person from the idea and helps to balance participation.

If your team is computer-literate, investigate groupware that can help automate these processes. General guidelines for brainstorming:

- Generate as many ideas as possible. (Research indicates that the first 15–20 ideas are the ones everyone has already heard or tried. Go for more than 20 to increase the likelihood of innovation.)

- Don't comment on the ideas as they are generated. Even favorable comments can damage the process as it might shut down a person who had a differing idea.

- Encourage people to piggyback on earlier ideas. Variations are just as creative.

- Be sure to include some really wacky ideas. Admittedly they seldom make the final cut, but they are surprisingly valuable at sparking usable ideas.

**Weighted Criteria Matrix/Chart.** (Especially useful for step 4 of the process.) A weighted criteria matrix can be especially helpful in deciding from among a number of options. List the options across the top of the matrix. List the criteria or needs the options should address along the side. Weight each criteria from 1–10, spreading out your ratings. Compare each option to the criteria and give it a score (either a 1–10 scale or use only a 1, 3, or 9). Multiply the scores by the weight. Add up the columns to get an overall score for each option. Figure B.5 shows an example of a weighted criteria matrix.

| Criteria | Weight | Option 1 | Option 2 | Option 3 | Option 4 |
|----------|--------|----------|----------|----------|----------|
| Quality | 10 | 1 **10** | 10 **100** | 8 **80** | 3 **30** |
| Cost | 1 | 10 **10** | 5 **5** | 1 **1** | 7 **7** |
| Satisfact. | 7 | 7 **49** | 6 **42** | 10 **70** | 1 **7** |
| TOTAL | | **69** | **147** | **151** | **44** |

**Figure B.5**   Example of a weighted criteria chart.

# CLARIFYING TRUST VALUES

**Level:**        **Within teams, between teams, and institutional**

**Component: Commitment**

## Description

Common commitment is based on a shared set of values. Getting at those shared values is sometimes hard because we seldom examine our own values and often assume everyone holds the same ones. This exercise will stimulate a conversation about the values at play in your organization. By using situations (real or fictional) you can assess whether the actions taken (or likely to be taken) in those situations express the espoused values your organization claims to live by.

## How to Use

Print up a set of situations. Use the samples provided following or create some that more closely fit your organization's experience. Read through the situations one at a time. For each situation answer the following set of questions. [Note: if your group is large, you may want to print multiple sets and divide the groups into teams of 4–6 people.]

- How have we handled similar situations in the past? (Be honest.)
- What values do those actions exemplify?
- Are those the values we think we should be modeling?
- If not, what values should we model and how should we handle this type of situation in the future?

## Sample Situations

- Almost everyone on your team is extremely busy. However, there is one team member, Bill, who does not appear to do as much as everyone else. Bill has also made some mistakes in the past. Your team has just been asked to take on a new task that could logically fall under Bill's job description and role. Who do you give the task to?

- You are in the midst of an important project for one of your customers that could dramatically improve service to all your external customers. The project is due at the end of the week. Your leader just called and asked you to run a special report (that does not seem as important as the work you are currently doing) and of course, he wants the report by the end of the week. You don't have time to do both. What do you do?

- Your team does a task that your customers have asked for, but in the grand scheme of things, is not that important to the organization. This keeps you from having the time to do more important work. What do you do?

- You have been required by regulations to do a process in an inefficient way. It requires a great deal of paperwork and time that doesn't have a corresponding payback. Basically, there are a lot of non-value-added steps in the process. What do you do?

- Your customers have always thought of your team's role as one of paper pushing and grunt work. When you ask your customers what they most want from you, they emphasize these tasks. You feel that there is a lot more value that your team could be providing (such as being more consultative). What do you do?

- One of the tasks your team does could probably be done cheaper and as well by an outside vendor. This task requires the equivalent of one full-time person. So if you outsourced the task, at least one person on each team could lose their job. What do you do?

- During a team meeting your manager learns that the team will miss an important deadline for a customer. This is not the first time this has happened. Those involved with the project say that they will do their best.

- Your manager gets an angry call from your customer. The customer is furious over the service they received.

- Your team comes up with a very significant process improvement idea that saves the organization thousands of dollars.

- When confronted about a task left undone, a team member responds, "That's not my job."

- Another team has a big beef with your team. They complain to your manager.

- A high-level manager makes a significant and obvious error in judgment.

# RETOOLING FOR ORGANIZATIONAL TRUST

| | |
|---|---|
| **Level:** | **Institutional** |
| **Component:** | **Willingness to invest, examine assumptions, and risk** |

## Description

Sometimes the things holding an organization back from creating a trusting environment are right in front of you. This exercise is designed to help people identify and then challenge practices, structures, and policies that both encourage and discourage a climate of trust.

## How to Use

Convene a representative group of people from your organization. We have successfully done this activity with groups as large as 70 people. Divide the group into workable-sized subgroups (usually 4–6 people).

Assign each third of the subgroups responsibility for analyzing one of the following aspects of an organization:

- The culture—the norms (both spoken and unspoken), the rituals, the symbols, the climate of honesty and openness, the shared values (that is, risk taking, employee relations, customer relations), and so on.

- The structure—roles and responsibilities, reporting structures, control structures, reward/punishment policies, hiring and promotion policies, decision processes, and so on.

- Leadership—management philosophy, capability, honesty and integrity, accessibility, and so on.

Ask each group to answer the following set of questions:

- What do organizations do within your assigned category that destroy trust?

- What do organizations do within your assigned category that create trust?

- Which of the items on your list are true for your organization?

- What steps could your organization take to leverage the trust-building items?

- What steps could your organization take to fix or mitigate the trust-destroying items?

This process is especially effective when coupled with the use of the organizational trust assessment in Appendix A. A key is knowing where the institution currently resides in its trust development prior to seeking change. Just jumping into trust improvement action plans may be counterproductive without a good understanding of what is working and what is not.

# REFORMULATING FOR TRUST

**Level:** **Institutional**

**Component:** **Willingness to risk**

## Description

Reformulating a whole organization to encourage trust is no small undertaking. The process described here enables an organization to develop a comprehensive plan for action. The process requires between six and eight hours of work using a cross-sectional slice of the organization. We have successfully done this activity with groups from 5 to 50. The straightforward process of walking participants through building the "wall" described here can be best accomplished with a skilled facilitator. Utilize the skills of listening, time management, and subgroup processing. Do not be afraid to draw into the room people of passion and energy. It is much easier to create with such assets than bring into being something of value from compliant and lifeless followers.

## How to Use

The process involves completing each section of the "Trust Wall" (see Figure B.6). The order and instructions for each section of the wall follow.

**Trust Vision.** Create the vision of the trusting organization sought after. For the purposes of this activity, keep the focus of the conversation on trust. Use these questions to guide the conversation:

- What will this trust-filled organization look like?

- What will it feel like, taste like, smell like, sound like?

- What symbols will be present?

Go beyond merely an overworked written definition and make the vision come alive.

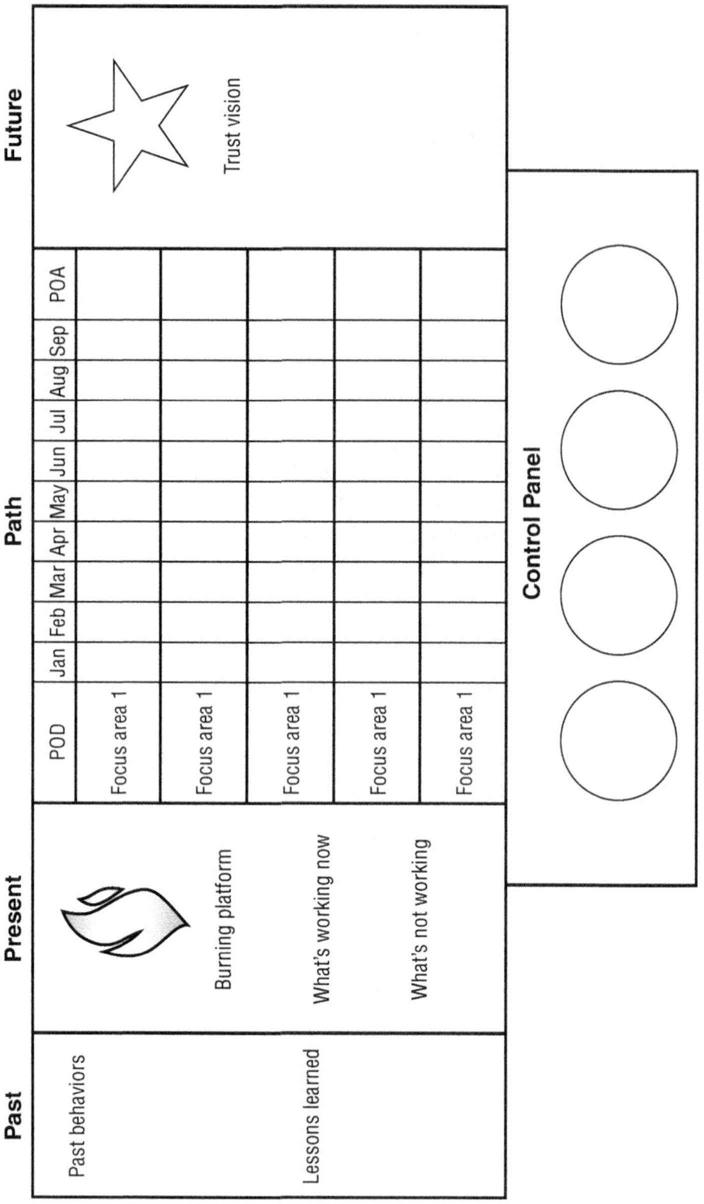


**Figure B.6** Trust wall.

**Control Panel.** How will improvements in institutional trust be detected? What are the control dials that point to change in the trust culture, structure, or leadership? Identify two to four key indicators of trust. Our Organizational assessment can be used as one of the tools. Others may include the average level of decision approval required, and incidents of theft or mismanagement.

**Burning Platform.** Why is a more trusting organization a necessity? Bring to mind a wooden platform burning at the edges. What calamity would occur if trust were not addressed? What is the cause of the fire? What is creating the urgency to change to a more trusting environment? Without a clear and compelling reason for change, the trust vision will remain unrealized.

**Past.** Without agreeing upon chapter and verse of the history of the organization, what actions have been taken to support trust? Likewise, list the past actions that have been seen to create distrust. Do not attempt to reconcile the input. People will view the same action in different lights.

**Lessons Learned.** Take the past experiences generated above and drive to the few key (5–8) lessons learned. The need to agree on the past is not as helpful as simply agreeing upon the truths of the different experiences. These truths will be more readily agreed to and provide a platform of mutual understanding.

**What's Working/What's Not Working.** List the assets and liabilities to creating trust in today's environment in the present tense. Change initiatives, the reworking of the reward system, or restructuring for business unit alignment are examples of current happenings that can affect the plan to develop trust.

**Focus Areas.** Determine the few, key focus areas through which trust will be built. What categories will yield trust when addressed? After identification, get clear on the point of arrival, or how you will know these focus areas have been achieved. It is our belief that when these focus areas are accomplished, the control panel will indicate improvement. Develop a time line of actions and accountable agents.

# Index